"Have you ever dreamt of finding that cherished mentor who truly wants you to live your best life? The one who has walked her own wild path and gathered a lifetime of wisdom along the way? The one who will share with you all her gifts and creativity and do it in a way that allows you the space to find your true direction?

Look no further! Lenore Kantor has written a generous, magical book to support your journey to finding the life you are looking to live. Playful and serious, deep and fun, this book supports profound exploration. You can feel you are in the presence of someone who has walked her talk.

In this world where every other person is professing to have the answers, it is so refreshing to find the real deal. Lenore is it!"

— Ann Bradney, Director, Radical Aliveness Institute

"In her new book, *So, What Do You Do?* Lenore shares no-nonsense career development strategies and advice with a blend of what she calls *Authentic Alchemy* – a pathway to personal vision as the foundation for each of us to build a future with purpose. Lenore Kantor does great work supporting our Bard MBA students on their career journeys, helping them find impact-oriented work in ESG finance, sustainability consulting, circular fashion and consumer goods, mission-driven start-ups and nonprofit management. Her voice shines through, making the book very readable and combines different spiritual insights to create a pathway for the personal growth process."

— Dr. Eban Goodstein, Director,
MBA in Sustainability at Bard College

"The *last and only career guide* you will need for meaningful work."
— Libby Dubick, Dubick & Associates

"This book is the perfect blend of expansive creative awakening and hard-earned wisdom that can guide anyone looking to identify and create a fulfilling career path. It's comprehensive as a guide, yet flexible based on your personal path. While everyone's life journey is unique, these tools will serve you well on your journey. Though I'm blessed to have created a career beyond my wildest dreams, a manual such as this would have saved me a lot of struggle along the way."

— Dana Claudat, founder of The School of Intention Feng Shui and The Tao of Dana

"Lenore Kantor has developed a unique and empowering guidance system to integrate your personal and professional lives, helping you to connect with your purpose and the work or calling that most fulfills you. Full of wonderful imagery, archetypal insights, deeper journey work, helpful analogies, and constructive ideas— she additionally suggests talismans and other time-honored rituals and tools to help you delve deeper into your truth and ignite the fire that drives you. A constant guide through your journey that can open you to new ideas, and help you release what holds you back, this is a book to take your time with and revisit whenever you feel stuck."

— Laurelle Rethke, author of *Connecting with Crystals: Crystal Wisdom and Stone Healing for Body, Mind, and Spirit*

"If you're ready for meaningful change in your life for clear vision with the tools to back it up, this book was written for you. Kantor shares her extensive experience and compassionate wisdom as she guides you to find your purpose in life in an open, engaged, and dynamic way…step by step. This guide is well organized and easy to follow, plus I always appreciate books with illustrative visuals and graphics, which there are plenty."

— Katrina Wynne, MA Transformative Tarot Counseling™

SO, WHAT DO YOU DO?

The Authentic Alchemy Path to Find Who You Are

LENORE KANTOR

GROWTH WARRIOR

Disclaimer

By participating in, downloading, reading, or completing the content within this book, you understand that it is purely for educational, informational, and entertainment purposes only. Neither Growth Warrior Ltd. nor Lenore Kantor claims to be experts on tarot. While the content within this workbook explores the nature of mental health, wellness, and psychology, it is not meant to be viewed as therapy, therapeutic advice, health advice, or a form of mental or emotional treatment. Therapy and counseling are beneficial to many, and I recommend seeking guidance and treatment from trained professionals when necessary.

ISBN: 979-8-9916583-0-0 (Print)
ISBN: 979-8-9916583-1-7 (Ebook)

Cover Design: Victoria Heath Silk
Book designed and typeset in Caslon
by InsideStudio26.com

www.growthwarrior.co

SO, WHAT DO YOU DO?

The Authentic Alchemy Path to Find Who You Are

LENORE KANTOR

GROWTH WARRIOR

ISBN: 979-8-9916583-0-0 (Print)
ISBN: 979-8-9916583-1-7 (Ebook)

Cover Design: Victoria Heath Silk
Book designed and typeset in Caslon
by InsideStudio26.com

www.growthwarrior.co

*This book is dedicated to all the seekers, young and old,
spiritual or otherwise, who long to find their
path to greater purpose and wholeness.*

CONTENTS

PREFACE

Who hasn't been stopped in their tracks, like a deer in headlights, by the question, "So, what do you do?" As if we could ever encapsulate our complete being in some pithy five-word response. Yet, our Western society constantly reinforces and defines our roles (and, arguably our value) in life by the need to "do" something, as if we must perform some important function to survive and merit worthiness.

Feeling the need to effectively communicate our contributions and chosen roles (and the more impressive, the better) can engender so much frustration and insecurity. Not to mention the expectation to convey our significance with deep conviction, enthusiasm, and humility. That's a lot of unnecessary pressure, if our lives weren't stressful enough.

I believe we are better served asking more meaningful questions, such as …

- What lights you up?

- What do you care most about?

- How would you like to change the world?

- What gifts make you special?

This book is an invitation to go beyond narrow definitions of what you do, since you are so much more than a tagline, catchphrase, or carefully scripted elevator pitch. Understanding the deeper and more meaningful aspect of what drives you to seek fulfillment in your life and work is often overlooked and rarely emphasized in traditional career and job search books.

The Authentic Alchemy Path offers an unconventional approach to finding meaning and purpose—a transformational guide designed to help you find your truth. I'm laying it all out for you to discover your life path and design a route to happiness and fulfillment with no BS. This approach is the culmination of more than four decades of my experience across multiple modalities, from my own personal process and my work with hundreds of leaders.

This user manual offers a process to help you to find your life's work by discovering and reinventing yourself again and again, since we continuously reveal new aspects of ourselves as we grow and evolve. My desire is to help you reclaim your fundamental truth, your unique creative expression, and your magic. You are a work of art, woven from unique and diverse experiences. It's time to appreciate and own your amazing essence!

Some simple, yet radical, truths underlie the Authentic Alchemy Path. My core message is that there are no wrong decisions on your path to purpose, only choices that you make and experiences you can learn from. While you may not yet understand the meaning of your life and work at this moment, trust that everything has been and is continuing to unfold to support your growth.

You are already on your path!

Your path is your purpose.

There isn't one right path, only *your path*.

There are no mistakes, only learning experiences.

Every challenge you face is an opportunity for growth.

Doing your inner, interpersonal, and outer work is the path to fulfillment.

Your work in the world is to find meaning in your journey.

Too often, people decide they can't have what they want, and then they resolutely push themselves to do something else, all the while regretting what they couldn't or didn't achieve. I believe there is another way for you to have your cake and eat it too. You can create whatever you want for yourself with the right attitude and effort. If you are willing to figure it out and do the work, that is your path forward. You will know who you are, regardless of what you do. With commitment and exploration, your essence will reveal itself to guide your way.

You got this! Let go of the pressure to get it right, do more, and be better, smarter, or faster than exactly where you are right now. Our societal focus on positioning and action often overlooks the foundational act of true self-understanding. The embodied approach presented here goes beyond mindset and tactics to include a broader and richer set of internal resources (your instincts, intuition, emotions, heart, soul's calling, and energy) that can provide incredible support, along with spiritual and mystical allies for a creative and mythical perspective to expand your understanding.

By following the exercises, and contemplating the personal reflections and prompts, you will uncover your purpose and impact. Doing the work, releasing the past, and starting your inner exploration will help you intentionally discover the best choices for you.

Imagine enjoying your life-path journey as it unfolds, experiencing ease and joy in the process. This does not mean you won't face challenges; however, with knowledge and powerful strategies, you will be able to handle whatever arises, since you are ultimately responsible for all your choices and reactions.

You can choose your own adventure in life. If you're unhappy where you are, you can make different decisions.

There isn't a single perfect way to be, and no exact actions you must take, only your choices, which give you more control and power than you may realize.

If you don't believe in what you're doing, or your current life and work aren't working for you now, you can uncover what is keeping you from happiness and chart a new path through your choices and experiences. Embrace experimentation, and believe in yourself, to find more flow rather than feeling overwhelmed or fighting to survive.

Choose to see life's inevitable ups and downs as learning experiences rather than as obstacles. Face and move through any challenges with awareness to integrate and overcome any blocks. Learn to embrace change from a place of authenticity, weaving together a beautiful tapestry of your life experiences across your personal and professional lives to create more balance.

Thank you for finding this book! I hope it meets you where you are and helps you discover and share your gifts. You are a powerful creator who can choose the direction of your life and reframe your reactions, interpretations, and stories without being at the mercy of limiting beliefs and difficult past experiences. It's time to rewrite the rules and create new opportunities for yourself. No regrets!

I'm excited to see what you learn, how you evolve, and where you decide to go. To redefine who you are, not only what you do, let your path lead you on a big adventure! No excuses or blame allowed. You're in the driver's seat. Take the steering wheel and go on the most amazing journey of your life.

Be yourself, fully and completely!

— *Lenore*

INTRODUCTION

IS YOUR WORK WORKING FOR YOU?

Many of us fall into our work by accident, circumstances, or influences beyond our conscious awareness (from family, friends, mentors, media, broader cultural pressures, and our own projections). We're each expected to choose our track early on (in college, high school, or even elementary school). As if we could know what we want when we barely know who we are.

So, we make the best choices we can, whether out of convenience, expediency, or idealism. Responding to circumstances, we encounter different work environments and challenges, and then we can find ourselves out of sync with who we thought we were or how we want to be. Increasingly, we want to live in alignment with our values, but we haven't been taught how to do this.

In fact, a large majority of people feel completely disconnected and lack a sense of purpose or fulfillment in their lives and work. Between 50 and 85 percent of the workforce is unhappy with their work, depending on which source you follow (the Pew Research Center or Gallup; see the Additional Resources section). So, it's no wonder our career decisions are often made by default, rather than by design. Either we jump from job to job, seeking more money, satisfaction, and responsibility, or we get stuck where we are, then realize we're not where we hoped to be. It can be hard to know where to start or how to opt out of the rat race and get off the work merry-go-round. Finding purpose can feel like a game of hide-and-seek, searching for something meaningful, only for it to elude our grasp.

Often, in our push to get ahead, we compete, compare, or despair that we haven't made enough progress or achieved more. We focus on the end goal, rather than how we got there, often not taking time to consider what truly matters for our own needs. Of course, having a big vision is important (in later chapters, we will review how it can guide us), but constantly striving to pursue an idealized future outcome or holy grail is not the same thing as embarking on your path to purpose with the goal of growth and learning. The former will get you somewhere, anywhere, while the latter will lead you to what you are meant to do.

Instead of going within and taking the time to understand *who* you are; *what* you want, care about, and need; and *why* it matters, you might immediately decide *where* you need to be, then jump into figuring out *how* to get there. Or, worse, select a role simply to impress others. Just because something feels like forward momentum doesn't mean it isn't directionless. Our society often prioritizes action over intention, which is why we may choose to keep "busy" yet feel so unproductive.

While knowing where and how to make things happen (also known as "getting sh*t done") are important outer actions, they can bypass the more essential first three elements that require inner reflection and understanding. By only focusing on *which* area to consider, you may overlook more critical variables that can impact your choices, like *when* and *whether*. We will be considering all the above, so you will have a very thoughtful and strategic framework for any decisions you make.

You may be seeking a shortcut to find your life's work, but that's not what you will find here. And, while this book can be a fast track to clarity, it's not an instant solution. Any career book that offers a quick fix is doing you a disservice. Instead, we will explore all the factors needed to create a meaningful life and fulfilling work that can often get overlooked in the rush to find a job and make a living. This is a deep dive—a thorough examination of what you should be considering from the outside in (where most traditional career books focus), from the inside out (where we will start), and everything in between (all the steps connecting both, and how to engage with others).

In doing the personal reflections here, the Authentic Alchemy Path may be the last and only guide you will need to find a fulfilling career and life, now and in the future, when you may inevitably consider your next shift. Our desire for growth and change is constant—often by choice, and sometimes by circumstances. This framework connects your head, heart, soul, and energetic blueprint, and it offers multiple tools and strategies to take with you into the future so you can source wisdom, knowledge, insight, and intelligence from within, tapping into yourself to find the answers you seek.

How to Benefit Most from This Guide

Placing this work in context may help you assess whether and how it can support you, since this book and process may not be for everyone. The multiple perspectives below, ranging from practical and strategic to spiritual and esoteric, have informed my experience and are incorporated into my approach:

- Coaching empowers people to face change and transformation through practical actions.

- Business strategy provides marketing and creative solutions that produce results.

- Somatic and embodiment practices explore the power stored within our bodies.

- Modern feng shui examines how environments and outside energies influence us.

- Energy medicine practices, shamanic healing, and crystal healing honor universal spirit and the natural world, aspiring to raise consciousness.

The intention in all my work is to honor the Earth, build more caring connections and community, heal suffering, and help people relate with more love and respect toward each other, and most importantly, toward themselves. This guide offers simple, practical, holistic spiritual and nondenominational approaches to support you in finding your purpose.

Those primarily seeking quick answers to make money, get ahead, and move up the corporate ladder may not find the practical job search tools, strategies, and tactics for a more traditional job or career search process. Many other sources already offer this information. This guide has exercises and personal reflections to find your life path, and it is less focused on job search strategies, though practical tips are included. Any effective job search requires understanding yourself deeply, and that is the premise for this work.

For the seekers—self-identifying idealists, dreamers, creatives, introverts, renegades, nonconformists, highly sensitive people, or high achievers—who want to create a sustainable planet, I hope this guide finds you, so you can live in alignment with your values. It is intended for conscious leaders, soulpreneurs, and founders who care about others and the planet, are committed to their own personal growth, want to live by their values, and long to do something meaningful and make a positive impact in the world.

We need to improve the health of our world, ecosystems, communities, and societies, and be of service to others, working on issues that matter. If you care deeply about these things and want to bring your gifts forward, be happier, feel more fulfilled through your work, and leave a positive legacy, then what I've shared here is for you.

THIS IS DESIGNED FOR THOSE WHO:	THIS MAY NOT BENEFIT THOSE WHO:
• Seek direction and clarity about their calling • Are ready to create change • Are frustrated with the status quo • Sense a deeper purpose • Want more meaning, impact, and fulfillment • Are called to make the world a better place • Are idealists who also want practical strategies • Are spiritual, mystical creatives, and unconventional thinkers • Are willing to go through a process of discovery • Want to connect more with their passion • Hope to create a meaningful legacy	• Are impatient • Want easy answers and a quick fix • Seek classic, traditional career and job search strategies • Need résumé tips • Are driven exclusively to succeed, achieve, and get ahead beyond all else • Focus on completely rational approaches • Are disconnected from their intuition • Want a guaranteed playbook • Pursue a clearly defined career trajectory

Self-Trust Is Empowerment

The outer world offers much insight into what possibilities are available, and I strongly encourage you to do external research and exploration. *Only you can know what is right for you*, which means that you get to own every decision—good, bad, and indifferent. Since everything is ultimately your choice, your knowing should be sourced from within. This is the beauty and the challenge of self-agency; you get to decide your future, consciously or unconsciously.

The stories and opinions shared are for your consideration, as there is no one way to do anything. Stated another way, only you will know what is best for you based on your needs, wants, preferences, lived experience, and reality. Others may offer their perspective to inform your process, but you are here to uncover the deep treasures buried within yourself that are longing to be expressed.

You are a unique, creative, and powerful being, here to do great things! While we may not have met, please know that I see you and your magic. I want you to embrace your unique essence and identity that has been shaped by your experiences, background, and vision, to stand in your truth and have everything you desire.

Why the Authentic Alchemy Path?

We value *authenticity*. People, objects, and experiences that are the *real deal*—coherent, consistent, and clearly aligned, not fake or bullshit. With the advent of artificial technologies and media manipulation, we are seeking more truth and integrity in every aspect of our lives, from healthy food choices to trustworthy friends and news sources; from inspiring mentors, celebrities, and social media accounts to books, blogs, and podcasts that we can trust. We are constantly evaluating who to believe and rely upon with our limited time and energy.

Children are often authentic until experiences teach them to hide parts of themselves or adopt certain behaviors to elicit reactions in their caregivers. As we age, younger and immature ways of operating (like trying to please our parents or being fiercely rebellious) may become our default MO (modus operandi), then subsequently hinder our interactions with others (for instance, causing us to not have boundaries or possibly push others away). We learn to dissemble to get by, get along, and fit in; but, at some point, this can stop serving us, whether we realize it or not.

Sadly, our culture has become rife with inauthenticity, from politicians to organizations that act without integrity and say things that aren't true or don't reflect their actions behind closed doors to AI algorithms that make sh*t up. Ideally, falsehoods become exposed, because their harm and impact have so many consequences, from public relations disasters, layoffs, data breaches, disengagement, or damaging and destructive disclosures.

Individuals face similar, yet different, challenges in how to truthfully represent themselves. Few work environments encourage wholeness. Individual passions, hobbies, interests, and styles must often be kept private, separate, and closeted. It's hard not to become fragmented into distinct business and personal brands or identities, hiding large parts of who we are.

We may overidentify with our professional interests and constantly wear a "suit" (literal business armor) or act in certain ways, code-switching and speaking differently to get by. This can make it difficult to know how and when to bring our full selves to every aspect of our lives.

Authenticity doesn't happen by accident. It requires intentional integrity in words, thoughts, actions, emotions, and energy; otherwise, others sense that things are fake or "off." We experience dissonance and disconnection on an intuitive level when there are differences between what we see, hear, and feel. Authenticity feels more relatable. In our desire to know, trust, and believe others, we are drawn to those who share their truth and are "on," so we don't viscerally sense they are "off."

AUTHENTICITY
Align what you think, say, feel, and do with how you engage

- ✓ THOUGHTS
- ✓ EMOTIONS

INNER

- ✓ WORDS

INTERPERSONAL

- ✓ ENERGY
- ✓ ACTIONS

OUTER

Authenticity is the alignment of our inner, interpersonal, and outer experiences to engage with the world as an integrated whole. The diagram above illustrates how authentic expression mirrors the Authentic Alchemy Path's inner, interpersonal, and outer framework.

Alchemy causes change and transformation—turning a base metal into gold, literally and physically. The Authentic Alchemy Path is designed to help you release all aspects that are "not self," so your inner truth can shine through. You are gold; and your work is to have this inner treasure emerge and be seen. Doing inner work removes any masks, blocks, or ways we cover our truths, so we can shift and align our outer beings and desires to start manifesting our dreams and find fulfillment in the world.

My goal is to help you rediscover who you really are—*you* and your truth—and uncover your passion and purpose that may be hidden from denial or overlooked by daily distractions, lack of attention, or lack of focus. Together, we'll explore what may be keeping you from doing your work in the world. As you reclaim yourself, understand your ideal environment, and redefine what matters, you will gain a fresh perspective, see the world with new eyes, and embrace your unique purpose.

Your search for purpose can be an exciting and joyful adventure, rather than excruciating and painful as many career books and coaches can imply. A positive mindset and a spirit of discovery will set you up for success and make your experience even more meaningful. (More about this to follow.)

Since we all can benefit from hearing and learning from other perspectives, you will get a glimpse into my own journey and career evolutions, as well as stories and examples of clients, students, and mentees (with modified names and identifying characteristics to honor their privacy). May these different viewpoints resonate and illustrate potential challenges you may face, inspiring and illuminating the diverse paths available to success.

MY STORY

My long and winding path has had many spirals circling back and around. In short, I went from being an idealistic college kid interested in nonprofit work and hoping to make a positive impact in the world to becoming an MBA and financial technology corporate executive. I then left a senior marketing position at the height of my career to start my own consulting firm (something I had wanted to do for years but had avoided out of fear and insecurity), and then pivoted yet again to focus on transformational coaching.

Our lives are often multidimensional, not single-threaded. While my formal financial marketing "career" unfolded, I was simultaneously pursuing outside interests through volunteer work at arts organizations and coaching training. I did not envision how this parallel direction would expand into the intuitive coaching I do now, yet its genesis was much earlier when I had studied psychology in college but decided not to pursue it. It took me thirty years to return to something I cared for deeply when my empowerment coaching became a side hustle, and subsequently, the primary focus of my work.

The table below shows a rough overview of how my professional journey evolved. There are certain common undercurrents in my strengths (what I was good at) and themes (things I cared about). I've noted some key career transition points in bold and what prompted those shifts. Of course, encapsulating all of this is easier to consider in retrospect, yet it doesn't fully reflect all the nuances of my experience.

AGE/STAGE	CAREER FOCUS	STRENGTHS	THEMES
Early Twenties/ Early Career	• Cocktail waitress • Summer camp counselor • Psychology BA degree • Nonprofit career in community services • Nonprofit arts administration	• Career counseling • Social services • Arts and community development • Human resources • Operations	• Being of service • Counseling/ advising • Personal growth • Learning and development • Arts and creativity
Late Twenties/ **Career Transition**	**Left nonprofit to obtain an MBA.** I attended business school with the intention of becoming a nonprofit executive director but discovered operations management (people, processes, and systems), which is where I chose to focus. After a summer internship at a telecommunications company, I was recruited for a bank management training program and redirected my career completely.		
Making my mark	• Technology and innovation • Quality management • Banking • Strategic analysis	• Operations management • Process improvement • Strategy • Communications	• Innovation • Problem solving • Enhancing business processes • Strategic planning

Thirties/ Professional Growth	• Financial technology • International brokerage • Financial markets • Equities, options, and derivatives • High-growth businesses	• Product management • Marketing strategy • Branding • Go-to-market • Internal and stakeholder communications • Government relations	• Product design and development • Brand positioning • Launch and go-to-market strategies • Messaging and effective communications
Forties/ Midcareer	• Executive leadership • CMO roles • Foreign exchange	• IPO (initial public offering) • Mergers and acquisitions • Marketing strategy	• Growth strategy • Thought leadership • Team building
Late Forties/ **Career Transition**	**Left the corporate sector to start my own business.** More about my story follows below. I realized I was no longer fulfilled and decided it was time to start my own business - the most critical turning point in my career.		
Charting a new path	• Entrepreneurship • Financial technology clients • Accelerator mentoring • Launch strategy	• Outsourced marketing • Strategic consulting • Founder coaching • Self-promotion	• Go-to-market strategy • Branding and events • Building a business • Personal growth

Fifties/ **Career Transition**	**Shifted my business focus.** After a decade on my own, I shifted my focus away from consulting and into more transformational and intuitive coaching after completing energy medicine and shamanic healing training. I committed to writing this book to share my approach.		
Setting My Own Direction	• Soulpreneur • Author • Transformational coach • Speaker	• Leadership coaching • Energy medicine • Shamanic healing • MBA career advisor	• Intuitive guidance • Mentorship/ advisory • Writing/ communication • Spiritual growth

There are multiple recurring threads woven into my tapestry. I enjoy solving challenging problems and designing new products and services, then bringing them to market. My creative side excels in conceptualizing branding and go-to-market strategies. I naturally build and develop teams and mentor staff, which has led me to advise founders, leaders, companies, and MBA students around their growth strategies.

A personal interest in learning, growth, and development led me to continuously invest in training to build new skills across multiple esoteric practices and healing modalities including somatic embodiment work and group process facilitation, energy medicine, tarot counseling, modern feng shui, shamanic and crystal healing, and cacao ceremonies, among others. This deep work feeds my soul, is creatively fulfilling, and offers extremely powerful and meaningful value for my clients.

Writing and communication have also been through lines. I teach others how to present, sell themselves, and negotiate, and I have now written a book. These skills and more are employed in my coaching and work as a soulpreneur, healer, author, and speaker.

In returning to my heart, I think of my journey as having lost and found myself many times over. A childhood interest in art inspired my passion for museums and ceramics as a hobby, for instance. Other connecting pieces that may seem apparent now weren't always obvious to me at the time. I never anticipated returning to psychology, and yet, that interest clearly drove my connection to coaching. I know my path to purpose will continue to evolve as my interests develop and change (I like a bit of variety).

While I love my work and my life, it took me almost forty years after college to find this level of focus and fulfillment. I could say it's "better late than never," but that wouldn't acknowledge how I benefited from every experience of my journey, even though some periods entailed more struggle than I might have chosen.

The Importance of Defining Moments

Prestige, respect, financial rewards—check, check, check. And yet, I was missing meaning, purpose, and alignment in my work. Twenty years of corporate work were satisfying and challenging enough. I felt a sense of achievement leading teams, mentoring staff, launching new products, and traveling globally. Amid these many valuable experiences, there were disconnects. In my midforties, my life somehow didn't feel like me.

As a highly sensitive and creative soul in a family that did not value or validate feelings, emotions weren't safe because they were shut down or shamed. How ironic that I chose the extremely conservative, corporate financial services sector, a highly male-dominated industry that valued money and results above all else, frowning upon caring or sensitivity.

I quickly learned to suppress my intuitive side, to be "all business all the time." I managed to fit in and excel because my analytical mind was adept at trying to control circumstances. My communication and interpersonal skills helped me manage complex business challenges. The industry I inadvertently fell into valued many of my strengths yet required me to also suppress most of my values and natural gifts.

I grew up surrounded by independent professionals—doctors, lawyers, dentists, creatives, and nonprofit leaders—in roles that I valued and respected. However, I needed to pursue my own thing and went the corporate route after business school for its structure and stability.

After taking a high-growth company public, followed by a successful merger and acquisition, I left a meeting, went into the bathroom, and broke down in tears. I had hit a breaking point. It was clear I couldn't keep doing the same old thing—living a charade and keeping up a facade. The emotions I had been keeping bottled up for years finally burst out.

I had essentially been hiding many aspects of my true self, including my progressive interests in social service and the arts. The constant focus on numbers, performance, and work was exhausting and stressful. I'd had to cancel vacation plans to be available for a merger announcement and was constantly tethered to my cell phone to check and respond to emails at all hours of the night. Work had sucked up all my energy and joie de vivre. I longed for my personal interests to be more fully reflected in how I was living my life, and to have more spaciousness.

I had lost my ability to keep putting on a good face and pretending to be interested in issues that I didn't particularly care about. I had been engaged working at a smaller entrepreneurial business with 150 people, but the behemoth corporate entity with 50,000 employees felt bureaucratic and constraining. Constant meetings with little autonomy or authority to direct the strategy felt soul-crushing. The cracks in my castle walls were too large to ignore, and the building came crashing down around me. *This was my Tower moment.*

In tarot, the Tower card represents a significant falling-out, and the breakdown of an existing structure built on a shaky foundation. One of the most iconic Tower images, from the classic Rider Waite Smith tarot deck, shows people jumping headfirst out of a burning building, perfectly illustrating when one's world is falling apart.

My emotional breakdown was that critical turning point, a crisis I couldn't ignore and the breakthrough that I needed. It remains challenging for me to realize how long I soldiered in the corporate world living from the mind, denying my true feelings. That wake-up call initiated my journey from executive and warrior to soulpreneur and shaman.

While I had idealized running an independent business for years, it felt too risky and unconventional for me to consider. At that time, entrepreneurship was not actively encouraged or supported like the *Shark Tank* startup nation we live in now. A friend suggested hiring a career counselor to explore whether I had what it took to work on my own. Multiple personality tests confirmed I could do it, and additional private coaching helped me prepare to leave my corporate job.

Sadly, rather than trust myself, I felt the need for external reassurance to overcome my internal fears and resistance. I remember thinking, if I hated having my own business, I could always go back. Yet, making the change to follow my instincts and trust my intuition led me in a direction I would never have anticipated.

What Can You Learn from My Path?

I can't predict what your Tower moment will look like, since it can take many forms—a health scare, layoff, breakup, divorce, accident, or other existential crisis. And perhaps you won't need a breakdown to find your breakthrough.

I can confidently say that, whenever and however your Tower crumbles, it's not a bad thing (even if it feels like it at the time), because you can't know where you will end up. That is its own kind of magic, if you let it unfold. While you won't understand how it all will play out, you can prepare yourself to embark on the journey of your life. Just know that sh*t happens, and you have the capacity to deal.

From my vantage point now, I see the ebbs and flows and seamless interweaving of all the aspects of my background as I shared in the above table, even as some of the strands went hiding or remained unwound and dangling for years. Yet, most of my professional choices were often reactions to my circumstances, choosing the best option at the time.

I wish I had been more strategic, but that wasn't exactly how it went down for me. I was practical and developed important skills, yet my choices weren't particularly intentional in retrospect, though they may have seemed to be at the time. It was not at all apparent where I would end up or how my experiences would come together. It's hard to imagine more disparate perspectives than idealistic nonprofit dreamer, driven corporate finance high achiever, holistic transformational coach, and shamanic practitioner.

I share this to illustrate that you don't need to know where or how all your experiences connect, but you need to trust that the elements can create a compelling narrative when properly interpreted and fully understood. Making meaning from seemingly illogical choices can take time to coalesce. However, there were some rationale, values, and truths at the heart of your choices. Once you own and accept why things happened as they did, you can make informed decisions about where to go next. This is when you can become more conscious.

It wasn't until I started my own business that I felt empowered in a safer space to bring my full self forward. I have integrated the strategic and practical business expertise from all my experiences (leading, managing, running a business, mentoring others, spiritual exploration, and personal development) and used both my right and left brain to creatively inform my work.

My uniquely *"empathetic and no BS"* approach (as clients tell me) is shared throughout the book. I want to encourage and support you, while telling it to you straight. You can find your own path that is both pragmatic and magical; create wholeness, alignment, and integrity in your life; and work through awareness and action. Let this guide show you how to embrace your true self by integrating your intuition and all your experiences with love and compassion.

Lessons Learned along the Way

Here are some additional reflections on my journey that feel relevant to the book's teachings.

Starting my own business was an *intentional choice*, though many default to consulting after getting laid off, thinking it will be an easy way to earn income. That can be a miscalculation. Consulting required many adjustments, from not getting a steady paycheck to learning to sell myself (which was particularly challenging, even for me, an experienced marketer) and having to do most things myself without the backing of an established organization's brand or resources. I learned over time, but it was a process. *Don't underestimate the learning curve and time involved in important life changes.*

Free advice is sometimes worth what you pay for it: nothing. After starting my business, I received unsolicited input from multiple former colleagues who shared suggestions about how to market and promote myself or how they would do things differently. I initially took this feedback personally and questioned my choices, but later, I determined their opinions were simply their points of view, and not necessarily relevant for me. I had my own style and way of operating, and never followed someone else's playbook particularly well. I learned to not internalize criticism that didn't support my needs or situation. When someone shares their opinion now, I consider its value and carefully filter the input by considering the source. I encourage you to do the same and *be your own authority*.

I was fortunate to *discover my sweet spot* early in my career, a unique skill set of leading product management and go-to-market strategies for high-growth financial technology businesses. However, once I built the product, team, and processes, it was time for me to move on. While some marketers enjoy managing daily operations, that was never me. I preferred and excelled in high-growth, new product launch roles. I prioritized opportunities that met these criteria and immediately recognized when something would not be a fit. Knowing your strengths, preferences, and interests *establishes your distinct brand* and *enables smarter choices because you know what works for you.*

Leaving a large, established organization to run my own business required many new and unanticipated skills. I had to learn to *right-size my activities to focus on the important priorities*. Early business decisions reflected my corporate perspective, causing me to overbuild unnecessary structures that impeded my growth, and it took years to unwind those ingrained ideas. Eventually, I became more comfortable with uncertainty, released the need to control everything, and found more flow and creativity. *Recognizing where you are at, what to let go of, and when new skills are needed* is an important aspect of adapting to change.

Change is constant. After starting my business, I needed to *rebrand the company to better position my services*. My initial business name confused potential clients, but I resisted changing it for a year, attached to what I had created. Once I finally accepted that it was no longer serving me, I renamed my business Growth Warrior, to move in a new direction. Sometimes, *a bigger vision is needed to shift focus.*

I underwent yet another pivot after a decade of independent consulting work became unfulfilling. Disillusioned by the limitations of external advisory work, I shifted my focus to individual leaders, founders, and business owners, rather than organizations themselves. I was tired of trying to fit in a box, since my interests had evolved, and I wanted to expand in new ways. A strong and compelling internal voice was telling me I needed to make a change. *Listen to your instincts when they guide you in a new direction.*

Luck and Timing

Shortly before the COVID-19 pandemic, I was recruited for a chief marketing officer position. While I hadn't planned to return to a corporate role, the opportunity to grow a business, take a company public, and have a profitable exit was appealing. I received a verbal offer from the CEO, then COVID hit, and the company went radio silent. I had given a large consulting client notice, so that project wound down and I was left with a lot of free time.

While initially disappointed by this professional turn of events, I ultimately was relieved and grateful on a personal level. It allowed me to spend quality time with my father who passed several months later. Any demanding corporate leadership role would have limited my availability for him, so I interpreted this unanticipated outcome as a blessing.

I subsequently learned that tech company had experienced significant management turnover (replacing multiple CMOs and CEOs in four years), which I thankfully avoided. Instead, I had invaluable family time, prioritizing what mattered most to me. I share this because we can't know what circumstances will unfold, but if we trust that we are on our path, then we will be guided. Some things happen for reasons beyond our control and may take longer than expected to meet our goals.

Making Space for Change

In another life, I might have been an interior decorator or a product designer, since I love design. During the pandemic, I decided to pursue this passion by studying feng shui, which looks holistically at the energetic flow within an environment. Clearing and decluttering can refresh a space, and it has been cathartic for me at many stages of my evolution to release what I'd been holding on to but no longer wanted or needed.

When I feel stuck, I reevaluate which elements and objects I still value in my life, often revealing hopes, desires, or expectations that never materialized or are no longer true for me, symbolizing hidden beliefs of what I "should" do, have, or be. I will share more about how important this process can be in the chapter, "Step 0: CLEAR."

My ten-year business anniversary revealed overflowing file folders, drawers, and shelves filled with objects from my former executive life. One rainy weekend, I gathered everything I no longer identified with. My last remaining black pinstripe suit and high heels (symbolic representations of my power) that no longer fit me or my life had to go, since my personal style and needs had completely changed. I donated them and ditched financial M&A deal tombstones and other stuff that had been filling my house and taking up space in my mind.

I made a huge bonfire (safely) in my backyard and burned old business cards, marketing collateral, and other documents, releasing years of heaviness I didn't even know I was carrying. Watching the smoke rise as my old papers turned to ash gave me a sense of inner freedom and lightness, letting go to create new possibilities.

Reading the Tea Leaves

A year ago, I received a divinatory reading from a fellow shaman who saw two paths for me to pursue, both reaching the same destination. One path was long and winding, while the other was more direct. This insight echoed a previous tarot reading I'd received shortly after starting my business years earlier. That reader had foretold that I could keep doing what I had done, but it would take me longer to ultimately reach my goals and perhaps not be as satisfying.

I often unconsciously chose the longer, more circuitous path because sticking with the tried and true felt safer than throwing caution to the wind and taking a leap. I maintained my corporate connection, keeping my spirituality in the closet for years as I struggled to find a way to integrate all my interests. My resistance and those choices often prolonged my process. Clearly, I needed to experience certain challenges and learn those lessons.

Many times, I wished for a do-over for certain difficult decisions, but that was not my path. I know that every choice has made me who I am, and I have no regrets. Thankfully, these days, I'm faster at recognizing how I get in my own way. My intention with this guide is to give you a sense of purpose and clarity so you can move toward your vision more swiftly, while also recognizing that there are no mistakes.

When My Larger Calling Called

It was hard to ignore the voice booming in my ears.

"Let's go! It's time to stop f*cking around!"

These words came to and through me during a vision quest journey in Mexico this past year. The message was clear: I was being commanded to wake up and get moving, to start doing my work in the world in a much bigger way. I had to admit to myself that I'd been playing small, and it was time to stop dillydallying. There was too much work to do.

I've known my mission is to empower high-achieving, values-driven, and soul-centered leaders like you to find your path and purpose. This book integrates every tool in my arsenal, and there are many. My mandate is to share this wisdom more broadly and make it accessible, so you can step into your power and inner wisdom to make a positive impact in the world. My invitation is to believe you can connect your head, heart, and entire body to unlock your full power.

Connecting with your heart and soul, and doing your inner work, will save you years of searching for meaning and will give you the keys to finding your way forward with confidence and ease. Our society's disconnection from the Earth and each other has only reinforced my urgency to support conscious, caring, and purpose-driven leaders like you to redefine success and thoughtful growth to support a better world.

GUIDANCE

WHERE ARE YOU NOW?

AGE AND STAGE

This guidebook can support you wherever you may find yourself in your personal path and work trajectory. While the steps and process are universal, your life and work journey will be unique; depending on where you are right now, your focus may shift. Early on, it's important to gain as much experience as possible, then over time, you may shift toward growth and healing on your way toward clarifying a broader personal mission and legacy. Your desire to learn and adapt may ebb and flow as you focus on different life priorities.

Make the most out of wherever you are now. Here are some general considerations, depending on your stage of life.

- **EARLY CAREER (Twenties):** Starting your career presents an opportunity to make choices that can influence and direct your path toward what you want. At the beginning of your personal evolution, you may not know where to focus, so embrace experimentation and discovery to explore different avenues.
  - ¤ This phase is about trying to figure things out. Explore, and gain as much experience as possible, to learn and clarify what you do and don't enjoy. Define your values and understand what you care most about. This can be an exciting period to take risks without having other obligations and minimal downside, as some experimentation is to be expected.

- **MIDCAREER (Thirties and Forties):** With some experience under your belt, you can continue to grow and change to make smart and strategic choices about your future. In getting to know yourself better, and because of other life decisions, your priorities may change. If you find yourself off course or doing uninspired work, you can pivot into more purpose and meaning. Should family priorities arise, you may need to create more flexibility in your lifestyle. Own your passions and where you want to put your energy and attention. This is an important time to focus, if possible.

  ¤ Periods of change can reveal disappointment or dissatisfaction with previous choices. Know that more fulfillment is possible. Clarify what is most meaningful for you now. Recognize what's not working by uncovering your blocks and overcoming your limitations. Address and overcome any fears or resistance, reframe your story, and recognize what is needed to show up as who you want to be. This is a valuable opportunity to step into more authenticity and own your power.

- **LATE CAREER (Fifties, Sixties, and Beyond):** Professionals who have amassed significant experiences, either in specific areas or across diverse activities, can define how to spend their time with greater self-awareness and acceptance. Address any personal growth and healing work needed to resolve any challenges. Seek greater fulfillment in different areas of your life that may require redefining your working identity. Lose the regrets and go after whatever you care most about by overcoming any resistance.

  ¤ Give yourself permission to pursue what you care about and stop worrying about what others think. Be more of yourself, share your wisdom, and give back to others. You may have more time and space to pursue other interests and continue learning and growing.

Approaching one's seventies or later can be a time of eldership, a period of wisdom and contribution where you share your knowledge and perspective with others. If you haven't pursued your passions previously, now is the time. Use your energy to explore what brings you joy and what will light you up. Defining a personal mission and legacy, if you haven't already, can offer a renewed sense of purpose.

Below is an overview of each stage's focus, mission, priorities, and challenges.

STAGE	EARLY	MID	LATE
Focus	Discovery	Growth	Sharing
Mission	*Find yourself*	*Overcome and integrate*	*Be yourself and give back*
Priorities	• Get experience • Learn a lot • Clarify your vision • Define your values • Learn who you are	• Uncover your blocks • Work through fear • Reframe your story • Reclaim yourself • Own your power	• Create a big vision • Stop worrying • Pursue what you want • Share your wisdom • Consider your legacy
Challenge	*What is possible?*	*I want more!*	*Let's do this!*

These are merely guidelines to put things in perspective, rather than hard-and-fast rules. Each stage is important and builds upon the previous one, and your evolution may be unique. Midcareer or late-career professionals who think they need to scrap years of experience to remake themselves over from the beginning are not owning their strengths. I often remind them that this is not true or necessary if they understand their strengths and know what is important now.

Many younger, early-stage individuals have incredible clarity around their personal missions. Your process will be a function of your willingness to do your deep, personal work. You can make progress on your journey wherever you are by giving yourself grace, recognizing what is most important, and choosing to focus on activities that will move you forward.

Meaning beyond Money

Money makes the world go around, and it is essential to earn a living. Other books deal with scarcity mindset and forming a healthy relationship with money; here, we will help you uncover what gives you meaning. You get to decide how money fits into that overall equation based on your unique situation, needs, and desires.

Creating one's ideal life and work is a nuanced undertaking. Money is one factor among many influencing the search for fulfillment. In my experience, not everyone is solely motivated by financial incentives, and money alone will not bring happiness. Yet, we need a baseline to cover our core needs for safety and security. It can be easy to get caught up in the pursuit of income above all else (cue all the supposed gurus selling programs on how to earn "seven figures"), which can create mostly stress, selfishness, greed, shortsightedness, illness, and resentment.

This is not to say money isn't important, because of course, expenses and #life. My invitation is to look at all the factors you care about to design your life in alignment with your values and needs. In managing, hiring, mentoring, and promoting staff, I have seen many individuals focus primarily on their compensation, as if more money will make them happier, while overlooking the importance of other relevant factors like growth opportunities, training, leadership development, and autonomy.

It's also important to know your value relative to the market and your overall contribution, to find a fair balance that doesn't overestimate or underestimate your earnings. By knowing what is most essential to you, you can best assess the impact you desire and what compensation will support your longer-term goals.

Sure, it's easy to compare yourself to others who appear to be earning more, and your ego can take a hit. You must know your worth to stand in your value; however, that's not the full picture. You may also want to be respected, appreciated, valued, and seen for your contributions in other ways. To grow and learn; to be challenged, acknowledged, supported, and mentored; to feel inspired by the mission and impact of your work, contributing to a greater purpose and creating positive change in the world. Or you could do your own thing and live off the grid, completely outside the realm of corporate bureaucracy and traditional societal expectations. Each of these might be important for you at different times in your life.

For some, work is a place to find belonging, validation, and acceptance. No one tells their boss, *"Please give me the love I never got from my mother and father,"* yet, underlying psychological issues and personal dynamics often play out in professional environments without individuals realizing their impact. My coaching work helps clients understand their underlying energies, emotions, and experiences without getting stuck in stories. While this guidebook won't directly address various psychological issues that can come into play, it does call attention to personal and professional areas that may warrant further examination.

Take a holistic perspective to consider what you really need and want, examine what may be going on beneath the surface, and apply practical strategies. Remember that you are here to do great things. The Authentic Alchemy Path can help you create meaningful change and achieve what you want.

What You Can Expect

The Authentic Alchemy Path is meant to meet you where you are. Choose your own adventure. Decide which steps to follow, exercises to complete, and ideas that resonate. Do the activities that call you and recognize you will be learning simply by doing. Actively engaging with the process and reflections will help you get the most out of it.

Your path is yours alone; it's an "inside job." Live from your inner wisdom, letting your intuition guide you, rather than following outside influences and what others think, say, or recommend. While others may advise and inform you, no one else can tell you what to do.

Try not to outsource your choices to others. Gather information to evaluate, but don't relinquish your agency. I won't give you the answers, just lots of thoughtful questions and processes to uncover your own way. While many clients have paid me to give them a playbook, I prefer to help you uncover answers for yourself. Learn from my experience walking the path and the process of guiding many others like you to more self-awareness.

Form follows function, so your work in the world will reflect your inner, interpersonal, and outer work. By learning as much as you can about yourself, your path will unfold. While it can be easy to focus on searching and pursuing, what you are meant to do may find you in the least likely of places, so be aware that you may not need to go after it if you let it come to you.

You can't rush your healing.
—Trevor Hall

The more you learn and integrate your lessons, the faster your journey will be. Your ability to make sense of your experiences, how you choose to tell your story, and the choices you make all contribute to your process. In some cases, figuring out what you don't like will help you clarify what you do like, and that's valuable information.

Remember that your goal is to find the meaning in what you are and have been doing; to rediscover who you are after pulling back all the layers, defenses, illusory beliefs, demands, expectations, and comparison to let your truth come through.

Know that you and your hero/heroine's journey will be supported by a thoughtful structure and the calling of your soul. I see you and honor your willingness to face yourself and uncover your truth, and your desire to learn and grow, take risks, experiment, and trust yourself more. You are unique, and it's time to let your light shine!

HOW TO USE THIS GUIDE

This guide is structured to include multiple activities within each chapter to give you more clarity around your personal situation. These suggestions for growth work are intended to help you uncover more insight to inform your journey.

Within each step of the Authentic Alchemy Path are four primary types of work you will be invited to do, each of which helps you tap into a different aspect of yourself and may reveal different types of information, so I encourage you to try them all to see what connects. Together, they will help you to create positive change.

- *CHECK-INS* are reflections to consider, centered in your *mind* and thoughts.

- *PRACTICES* are actions to take, focused on *behaviors.*

- *EXERCISES* are intentions to set to connect with and unlock your *intuition.*

- *RITUALS* are processes to support your change, give you more clarity, and center in your *heart and spirit.*

Additional resources include *STORIES* from clients, students, or founders I've coached for examples and *inspiration* on how others have navigated similar challenges and to highlight aspects of the process or important points.

Each step builds upon the previous one as an important element of your journey, so I recommend going through the chapters in the order they appear. Skipping over the inner work on mindset and clearing to rush into the interpersonal work around messaging or the outer work around action may shortchange your process. Follow each step as indicated to avoid circling back.

Should you get stuck on a particular step, you can move forward to the next one. However, realize that your resistance may reveal some valuable information about where more personal reflection and examination is needed. Many individuals rush to pursue a new job because they're unhappy and want a change, only to discover they're not sure it's really what they want when they get there. The "one step forward, two steps back" experience is not uncommon. When you start speeding up, consider whether slowing down and examining what is really going on can uncover what you may not have been ready to explore previously.

The next chapter, "Authentic Alchemy Framework," outlines the overall framework, what to expect, and how to apply it. Corresponding to each chapter, you will find an overview outlining major aspects of the process. Graphical images include creative inspiration from myths, archetypes, and allies to support you, including tarot cards, colors, crystals, chakras, and elements, as well as positive affirmation statements and power animals that symbolize different energies. Alternative imagery can facilitate learning in different ways (seeing, doing, hearing, thinking, writing). Considering these archetypes can place your own journey in context to understand the bigger picture from another vantage point, if useful.

More background on how to work with these tools is explained in the chapter, "Creative Support for Your Journey." For instance, rituals are powerful ways to shift energy by getting beyond thoughts. Consider my suggestions a jumping-off point to create personal practices that work for you. If a chapter theme mirrors your journey, you could journal about your challenges or connect with the elements (for instance, using earth to ground; fire to cook with spices; or crystals for visual, energetic, and spiritual uplevelling). Use these allies however you see fit.

Consider doing as many activities as possible to inform your process as fun "pattern interrupts" to consider your approach with a fresh perspective. Try to get out of your head and beyond preconceived notions about what you "should" be doing. However, you may also find that some of the prompts feel more important for you than others, so focus on what connects.

Keep what resonates with you and ignore the rest. The suggestions provided are here to encourage playfulness and fun. Be open to new adventures and discoveries. Curiosity will help you uncover more synchronicities along the way.

Hard or Easy: You Choose

Change is inherently unsettling, and work can present many challenges and disappointments. Speaking from years of experience with bad bosses, highly stressful positions, nasty office politics, and other discouraging setbacks, I have also been fortunate to grow immensely and do thoughtful and creatively inspiring work.

Following and connecting with our hearts in our work can feel vulnerable and uncomfortable, and it may require us to face our fears, painful memories, or other unmet longings. Doing our personal work helps us understand ourselves and our relationship with power and others. Having this awareness allows us to leave the past in the past where it belongs and put our hungry ghosts to rest.

Above all else, I recommend being yourself. It is far easier than trying to be someone or something you are not, twisting yourself into knots trying to fit in and belong, or forcing yourself to do things you don't enjoy or care about. I've been there and done that. I get it; however, when you don't care about your work (or anything, for that matter), it kind of shows. It's obvious to others in your energy level and demeanor, and you will feel it inside. You won't be excited or inspired. Who wants to be burned-out and blah when you can be brilliant and on fire in a good way?

Any kind of change, let alone a deep search for meaning, takes time, so don't assume you'll hit gold overnight. Choosing to invest your time and energy into what you care about will start to pay off in ways big and small. Just reading this book will put the energy of change into motion. I promise! Your intention is that powerful. You will become enthusiastic as you connect more with what you care about, and that energy will motivate you to explore and discover new things.

Know that change can often evoke big feelings. Strong or ambivalent emotions can be interpreted either as stress, anxiety, and feeling overwhelmed, or as excitement, inspiration, and growth. The same underlying physical feelings can result in completely different responses and outcomes, depending on how you analyze your energy and choose to react. How will you react and then respond to your reaction?

Research has shown that seeing possibilities and acknowledging challenges in positive ways is more likely to support growth, while analyzing stress negatively can diminish health. Which perspective will you choose: stress and struggle, or excitement and expansion? Rather than defaulting to a negative outlook, consider reframing your perspective to see things differently.

Looked at another way, change can be a deep self-discovery and reclamation process to call back and integrate hidden or lost parts of yourself. Or it could be an evolutionary process of letting new and exciting aspects of yourself emerge. While change may feel uncomfortable at times, you can embrace the growth edges you feel, knowing that intense emotions and discomfort are natural parts of the transformational process.

Having this expanded perspective can shift your perceptions to let go of unhelpful old stories you may have told yourself. Rather than feeling stuck, broken, wrong, or helpless, consider that you are exactly where you are meant to be on the path to becoming more of yourself!

No, try not. Do or do not, there is no try.
—Yoda, *Star Wars*

Change Is a Verb and a Noun

We experience change, and we have the power to change ourselves, through our actions and outlooks. While behaviors are important, mindset also matters. Simply wishing something is true does not make it so. We hope that thinking about something will get us what we want. And, while focus is invaluable, we can attract more of where our energy is directed, sometimes in unexpected ways. Desire alone is not enough; work is necessary to create what we want! We need to show up, decide what we feel is most important, break through our fears and resistance, and go out into the world to learn and grow.

This effort and courage are not for the weak or fainthearted. And the payoff is worth it: more fulfillment, living a life of growth and purpose, knowing you haven't compromised your values or sacrificed your vision. I share the stories in this book to demonstrate how results come from personal reflection and awareness.

You will benefit from doing the exercises and practices and fully engaging your mind, body, spirit, and energy to create authentic alignment—making yourself whole. Your magic will unfold as you start the process, make new discoveries, and let the puzzle pieces click into place. In a few short weeks, I hope you will look back to appreciate how much has shifted and how much better you know yourself.

True change comes from integration and assimilation to embody a new way of being. Change is possible and will come as you discover what you are meant to be doing in moving through these practices and letting your process unfold. At a minimum, you will feel more connected to yourself, and that is where great things begin.

Recognizing how inherently uncomfortable change can be is liberating. It's not just you! Our bodies are biologically wired to resist change because unknown new or different things are perceived as dangerous. We naturally prefer security and stability. Keeping things the same, in stasis, makes us feel safe. In pursuing something new, you may experience unexpected reactions—internally from your own instincts and body, and externally, possibly from others who may want to keep things the same. Those closest to you may want you to remain how you have been because it makes their lives more stable and predictable.

In every moment, you can choose your experience. Will you lean into the discomfort and interpret it as excitement (with the positive energy of possibility), or will you pull back with overwhelm (feeling the negative energy of fear)? Whatever mindset you choose will determine how you experience the same emotional and physical sensations. When possible, I encourage you to choose excitement and anticipation, over anxiety and stress.

Hard and challenging work need not be painful, but growth happens through learning and transformation. Nothing meaningful will happen overnight. Uncovering, finding, and doing your work in the world takes courage, commitment, persistence, and passion—it is not a quick fix ... sorry.

Follow the Authentic Alchemy Path roadmap to empower you, support your growth, and point you toward your dreams like a recipe book, not a mandatory, prescriptive, one-size-fits-all methodology. Bakers can follow the measurements exactly, and scratch chefs can improvise to their personal preferences. Pick and choose what works for you and customize it to make it your own. Regardless, you are in exactly the right place to start your next adventure.

AUTHENTIC ALCHEMY FRAMEWORK

The Authentic Alchemy Path is intended to support your internal alignment amid ongoing change by coming back to yourself and removing all the barriers, blocks, and ways you have covered or hidden the truth of who you really are. Integrating all aspects of yourself empowers you to show up whole and grounded, free of expectations, comparisons, or worries about others.

Authenticity comes from having internal consistency and coherence as you connect your thoughts, words, actions, and energy. Your alchemical transformation allows a new state of being to emerge, and the increased awareness unlocks more possibilities. You will undergo a metamorphosis like a butterfly emerging from the caterpillar's chrysalis—from a goopy soup to a radiant being.

Your life path is to discover what truly lights you up by pursuing what you are meant to do. This is your magic. There is not one possible end goal, but rather, an ongoing evolution across your life stages, choices, actions, reactions, and attitudes. Every experience will offer you a lesson to learn from and integrate. Your unique journey will occur at your own pace. There's little value in comparing where you are to someone else, because their challenges and situation will be different from yours.

Learning to Do You

Let your passions be guides to help you uncover your true interests, values, and preferences, to create more alignment. Natural strengths and talents that you may have taken for granted should be leveraged fully because these are your gifts. However, just because you are good at something that comes easily to you doesn't mean you need to do that activity all the time.

My client, John, shared a powerful and unsettling realization. Many characteristics he considered to be personal strengths, such as being super-organized, diligent, and detail-oriented, were byproducts of old coping mechanisms he'd developed to navigate the world at a young age. Aspects of his family life were chaotic, and he'd learned to fend for himself by becoming highly analytical and methodical in his approach to solving problems.

While his skills were valued in his current work, he wondered if they had outlived their purpose as John noticed he was perpetuating defensive and self-protective strategies that were exhausting. This awareness became the impetus for his need to make changes and consider a new professional path based more on his true interests and desires. His personal work involved unwinding old patterns and rewriting unhelpful beliefs to better support how he wished to feel in the future: confident and capable, rather than anxious and defensive.

Ideally, you will find a balance between what you truly enjoy and want to do versus what you can do and feel you must do to get ahead. As you understand your true needs, it will help you to *know, trust, and be yourself more of the time.*

Some ways you can be more yourself are to:

- *Listen* to and follow your inner wisdom.

- *Notice* and appreciate when synchronistic signs and symbols occur.

- *Feel* your full body experience, without ignoring or denying what you notice.

- *Observe* the ways you choose to avoid conflict or differences.

- *Recognize* when and how you compete, compare, or try to structure your life in relation to others (peers, family, mentors, or broader capitalistic societal values).

- *Reflect* on your core values, vision, and mission—and return to yourself.

- *Slow down* to allow time for personal reflection and grace to guide you.

- *Breathe and ground* when you feel uncentered or overwhelmed.

- *Remember* that you are making progress through your choices, even when it may not be apparent.

Redefine Success on Your Own Terms

We all want to be loved and admired; however, seeking outer validation from others is not the route to deep, inner fulfillment and purpose. *You must walk your path alone.* Of course, we may be accompanied by partners, spouses, close friends, and family that we care about. In fact, companions are valuable support for your process. However, worrying, competing, and comparing yourself to others will not lead you to happiness; instead, it will take you to the land of lost dreams. I know because I almost landed there.

Growing up, many of us idealized the lives our parents lived, or perhaps we admired the stability that other friends' families had. Did you aspire to own a suburban house and have 2.2 kids, a nice backyard, and a picket fence? Or perhaps you wanted a luxe loft apartment in a city, with a view and a designer dog. At various points, each of these appealed to me until I needed to create my own vision. Others' versions of "success" can be lovely dreams, but we can't know the full story and what narrow parameters, implicit expectations, and limitations they involve.

At some point, we must recognize any self-imposed fantasies, and call them out for what they are, so we can find our true path. What works for others may not be right for you, even if it's what you aspired to in the past. Be aware of ways you seek external validation, compare yourself to others, or perhaps judge yourself.

Know what you value, so you can make conscious choices without needing to live or live up to someone else's life which was likely based on different values and priorities. You can choose the life you want to live based on your unique needs and desires, not on the expectations or experiences of others.

The Path Is the Process

Fundamentally, the Authentic Alchemy Path recognizes your unique journey. Too often, we confuse the ends (a desired outcome or result) with the means (how to achieve it). Consider reframing your experience so the path and journey matter the most. Focusing exclusively on the ends and your goals is beside the point.

Of course, goal setting can help clarify your vision and direct your actions; however, try to hold your goals loosely until you have validated that they are, in fact, what you want. Allow yourself to question your underlying assumptions about what is most important.

Trying to control your outcome and make decisions mainly from your head risks overpowering your heart and desire to find more meaning. You will find more ease and pleasure by undertaking your path with the desire to enjoy and learn from the process, to have the full experience.

Consider four different approaches to your path. Which will you follow?

- **Renegade:** Rejects others, and sometimes yourself, to be different.

- **Retrograde:** Does what others want and expect.

- **Rebel:** Discovers the path not taken to create something new.

- **Real:** Connects within and across lived experiences to find meaning.

You may undertake each of these paths at various points. I know that, at different stages of my life, each approach held its appeal.

Western culture idolizes work, whereas many Eastern cultures honor community. Some Indigenous societies recognize each person's unique spirit. Our society can define individuals by their work from ages twenty-five to sixty-five, though we often look outside ourselves even earlier for approval.

We could choose to reject what we see to become counterculture, where innovation and discovery can happen. Maybe move to the woods, live off-grid, and become a hermit. But, if you value relationships and connection, you might need to find another way to engage to stay in contact with civilization. As a former city girl who moved to the country, I recognize when I need urban energy in my life.

Our passions can set us free when we give ourselves permission to follow our interests rather than hiding who we are, what we love, and what we care about. The more we recognize our truth and acknowledge our needs, wants, desires, and capabilities, the faster we can feel more satisfied.

The Authentic Alchemy Path

The Authentic Alchemy Path encompasses eight steps to create true transformation that have evolved from my coaching and work over more than three decades. This path encapsulates that process as a framework to guide your journey and support your process. As noted, I recommend following the steps in order; however, some steps may occur concurrently. You may also review or revisit steps as you develop more clarity and face new challenges.

- *PREPARATION:* Before embarking on any journey, it's important to do some prework to set the stage for the larger process you will be undertaking. Here you are going to *set your objectives, prepare your mindset, and develop a plan to maximize success.*

Discovering your work in the world will entail navigating three primary phases:

- *INNER WORK* is the starting point. You go within to reflect on your own experience to understand your intentions, desires, strengths, and challenges. The goal of this phase is to *figure out who you are and clarify what matters to you.*

- *INTERPERSONAL WORK* helps place you in connection with others. As you learn to share your vision, you will *communicate and engage more broadly with others* from an integrated and evolved version of yourself.

47

- *OUTER WORK* is the final stage. It brings together all your learnings, so you have a solid foundation of wholeness to build upon. You will take definitive actions to *bring your dreams into reality and start manifesting* more of what you want.

The diagram on the next page illustrates how the steps relate to each other with more detailed descriptions following, and *how these relate to the design of a beautiful garden*. While I'm a reluctant gardener, I love the metaphor of plants and the natural world's lessons to support our growth process.

AUTHENTIC ALCHEMY PATH
FIND YOURSELF TO CREATE MORE FULFILLING LIFE & WORK

PREPARE

0

CLEAR

INTEND & PREPARE

INNER

1

REALIZE

DISCOVER & SEE

2

RELEASE

CLEAR & ALLOW

3

RECLAIM

TRUST & INTEGRATE

INTERPERSONAL

4

REFRAME

AFFIRM & SHARE

5

REIMAGINE

CLARIFY & FOCUS

OUTER

6

REVEAL

ACT & CONNECT

7

REAP

BE & DO YOU

PREPARATION (Top Row)

Step 0: CLEAR:

Thoughtfully plan to begin your process. Prepare to undertake your journey by setting clear intentions and creating a supportive physical environment. Create more open space for your new path by decluttering and performing other practices to remove physical and mental obstacles that may be blocking you from moving forward without restrictions.

» *Identify and prepare the area to plant your garden and start to prep the space by removing large rocks. Choose the right season to start your planning.*

INNER WORK (Second Row)

Step 1: REALIZE:

Become aware of your experience. Consider what you desire (in the future) and evaluate where you are now (in the present), to see what is true. Understand and assess your full situation.

» *The spark of inspiration arrives; you imagine being surrounded by lush greenery. Envision your garden landscape layout, and plan considering how you want to feel. What motivation is calling you to create your garden? Whether visualizing internally or drafting a written blueprint, intentionally assess your goals.*

Step 2: RELEASE:

See what may be hindering your progress. Notice what has been getting in the way of realizing your vision (by addressing issues from the past). Recognize when, why, and how you may be holding yourself back to remove blocks and let go of limiting beliefs, unhelpful behaviors, patterns, or experiences that are no longer working. Lighten your burden so you can move forward unencumbered.

» *Prepare your ground. Till the land to dig up any weeds that may be crowding out the space and compost the soil to make it healthy for new growth. Fortify the soil to ensure it is ready for seedlings to grow.*

Step 3: RECLAIM:

Integrate disowned parts of yourself to come back into wholeness. Stand firmly in the vision of who you need to be to realize your dreams, creating space for new opportunities.

» *Consider what you want to grow and where, and how you can use existing plantings you already have and incorporate new crops and shrubs. Recognize the season you are in. Winter may require waiting and planning, while you might not see your seeds are growing underground. In spring, new buds begin to emerge because of your previous efforts. Becoming more familiar with your terrain helps you prepare for what you wish to plant.*

INTERPERSONAL WORK (Third Row)

Step 4: REFRAME:

Uncover your truth. Develop and refine your internal narrative as you begin to share more broadly with others. Build a positive mindset to tell a new story that aligns with your intentions.

» *Formalize your planting strategy by choosing and identifying what you want to grow (for instance, annuals, perennials, herbs, bushes, or trees). What story are you telling through your garden (for instance, lush and wild, planned and minimalist, or practical and functional)?*

Step 5: REIMAGINE:

Envision how to move forward now. Begin making new and aligned choices with ease. Focus on what you know is possible to start moving forward.

» *Identify and optimize your plantings within the terroir and soil location. Give your garden the ideal sunlight, track the rainfall, and assess temperatures so it can prosper and grow.*

OUTER WORK (Bottom Row)

Step 6: REVEAL:

Discover who you really are. Own your inner wisdom. Ground and embody how you wish to be in the world and take intentional action.

» *Watch the fruits of your labor blossom as your plants grow. Sunflowers point toward the sun and start shedding their seeds for the next season. Some plants will multiply and expand under the right conditions, while others will need more water or sunlight.*

Step 7: REAP:

Become fully centered within yourself. Shift into presence and being. Celebrate, and approach your life and work from a place of wholeness, integrity, and joy.

» *Harvest the beautiful plants and flowers from your garden. Enjoy the outcome of all your effort and investment. Prune any overgrowth and prepare for the next season.*

How to Approach Your Discovery Process

The world is a book, and those who do not travel read only one page.
—Saint Augustine

As you embark on your journey, consider your approach to travel. Do you prefer to pack heavy, anticipating everything you might need so every option is covered? Or do you only take a light carry-on, giving you the flexibility to avoid baggage claim and change your plans on a moment's notice? Do you design a formal itinerary to see certain sights and highlights, or do you go rogue and follow where the day takes you, discovering things along the way and reacting to the situations and opportunities at hand?

Both approaches are valid and depend on the length of your trip, your planned activities, and your ultimate destinations. A former heavy packer, I've learned to travel light with only a carry-on to avoid checking a bag, so I have more freedom. I do some preliminary research to develop an itinerary with a list of things to see, so I can familiarize myself with my destination, then I adapt and respond to how I feel in the moment. This lets me adjust my plans to the weather, availability, and other opportunities that present themselves. While I rarely see everything on my list, I enjoy knowing what options are available and consciously choosing what feels most important for me to experience in the moment.

Both practicality and intuition are woven throughout this guidebook to help you navigate your way. The Authentic Alchemy Path steps are your high-level plan, and the resources offer additional options or excursions along the way. You are *"choosing your own adventure,"* since this is your life, after all. Chart your own path, knowing there are no wrong turns, only lessons to be learned.

Approaching your soul path journey as an adventure encourages learning from every experience along the way. On your path are many roads. You get to choose the directions, turnoffs, and stopping points you take as you look forward to enjoying your journey.

CREATIVE SUPPORT
FOR YOUR JOURNEY

In seeking your purpose, you are undertaking a broader mythical hero/heroine's journey, going beyond your head and heart to find deeper meaning and connection to your higher calling. Look for the synchronicities along the way. We've already explored the practical activities in each chapter: mindful check-ins, exercises, practices, and rituals.

In addition, mystical, spiritual, and heart-centered alternative references are included to place your process in the context of a larger quest for meaning, if you are so inspired. These are intended as counterpoint or adjunct references for those seeking to do deeper personal reflection. These invitations appear collectively in the diagrams included with each step of the process and may be used to inform your journey.

Additional Guidance for Your Process

Use these sources to enhance your personal growth work and broaden your understanding. I will share examples of how you may use them and how I have benefited from these different perspectives, philosophies, methodologies, and technologies in my own process.

Multiple diverse Eastern and Western lineages have informed my background from traditional somatic and psychotherapeutic modalities based on Charles Jung, John and Eva Pierrakos, and Arnold Mindell to Indigenous traditions like the Mayan cosmovision, Q'ero shamanic lineage, and Eastern practices like feng shui, yoga, Ayurveda, and Reiki, among others. My intention is to honor the spirit of what is shared in ways that may complement and enrich your experience. I do not believe there is "one way" to do things, and you may wish to customize the approaches shared here to what most resonates with you. Your own personal or cultural mythologies may be more meaningful and relevant, so let them inform your process.

Whatever perspective you bring, these resources are meant to offer inspiration and additional guidance. Included is some high-level, but by no means exhaustive, background on each aspect and how and why these may be of value and offer insight. There are practitioners who work with one or multiple areas for healing purposes. In my work, I sense what clients may need, and I follow their lead. As such, these resources are being presented collectively so you may explore unexpected connections or find possibilities that emerge between different related themes. They may inspire and fascinate you, be difficult to understand, or seem completely unrelated to your process. Please take what works for you and leave the rest.

As shared before, the Authentic Alchemy Path's eight-step process is based on a fundamental correlation between all aspects of our minds, bodies, spirits, visions, intuitions, energies, emotions, and environments. You will see these themes woven in the references shared here.

Chakras

Within Western psychology, you may be familiar with Maslow's Hierarchy of Needs, a framework that often presents individual needs visually within a pyramid, moving from physiological requirements at the bottom, through safety and security, to love and belonging, then to self-esteem, with self-actualization at the top. Maslow's framework mirrors many aspects of the chakra system from the root, the base and sense of grounding, through the crown and connection to meaning and the divine.

Chakras are spinning wheels of energy throughout the body's central meridian that support health and well-being. They are recognized by millions of people across many diverse traditional Eastern energy medicine practices from yoga, Ayurveda, and Hinduism, as well as traditional Chinese medicine and Qigong, as well as other holistic approaches. In chakras that are balanced, energy flows naturally and supports optimal health. Blocked chakras represent disrupted energy flows within the body and can create imbalances that, if unaddressed, can lead to illness over time.

The chakras are an important element within energy medicine, shamanic healing, and crystal healing practices to help identify unhealthy patterns in the body physically, energetically, emotionally, spiritually, and mentally. The specific chakras often correlate to underlying issues that may be occurring in one's outer experience. Releasing the stuck energy can support healing, build inner alignment, and create subtle shifts. Bringing awareness to imbalanced elements can create more flow in areas that are not always obvious to an individual's consciousness. Balanced chakras enhance energy and wholeness, facilitating greater embodiment and connection with the Earth.

As such, the seven primary chakras from root to crown, plus the soul star, are foundational elements of the Authentic Alchemy Path. More chakras exist and are recognized within different energy systems.

Connecting with the chakras physically or energetically is not required to do this work. Just as you don't need to know the ingredients of every food you eat to enjoy it or benefit from its nutrients, but those who love cooking might want a deeper understanding of the underlying recipe and seasonings for their own edification.

The more important awareness is around noticing whether your challenges exist around your thoughts (which could connect to your crown chakra) or your personal power (which would relate to your solar plexus) or some other area. By noticing what part of your body and energy field is constrained, you might also see if this relates to any physical ailments or experiences. Using the examples above, do you get headaches from overthinking, or tightness in your stomach around stress from work? These are helpful clues about chakra centers and areas of your body that are calling for your attention.

The chakra system can powerfully represent and reflect larger underlying patterns. Seeing the interconnectedness of our minds, bodies, spirits, emotions, and energies is also helpful.

The table below connects each chakra and its related color, focus, and description to the Authentic Alchemy Path steps. These are then correlated to the eight steps, with the far-right column showing how the guidebook activities also support and align with the chakras, offering holistic and multidimensional practices for wholeness and integration.

For instance, the third eye is blue and is related to your mind and beliefs which is the primary focus of Step 1: REALIZE. The check-in questions are an opportunity for you to reflect on your process and examine your thoughts more. You may find the full process diagram on page 49 to be a helpful reference.

This framework goes beyond mind/body awareness, since we benefit from the full integration across all aspects of our body (heart, and instincts), intuition, energy, and spirit.

#	Chakra	Color	Focus	Description	Step	Guidebook Activity
8	Soul Star	White	Consciousness	Access to your higher power	**0: CLEAR** Prepare and Intend	**CLEARING:** Review and release of old energies
7	Crown	Purple	Spirit/Beliefs	Trust in the universe and mindset	**7: REAP** Be and Do You	**RITUALS:** Mythical ways to shift your awareness
6	Third Eye	Blue/Indigo	Vision/Sight	Ability to envision possibility and see what's true	**1: REALIZE** Discover and See	**CHECK-INS:** Reflections on your situation and beliefs
5	Throat	Turquoise	Voice/Message	Stories and narratives you tell yourself and others	**4: REFRAME** Affirm and Share	**AFFIRMATIONS:** Positive words to support your mindset

4	Heart	Green/Pink	Belonging/Passion	Connection to yourself and others	3: RECLAIM Trust and Integrate	EXERCISES: Set intentions to create motivation
3	Solar Plexus	Yellow	Power/Action	Own your instincts, trust your gut, and act	6: REVEAL Act and Connect	PRACTICES: Take actions, and notice behaviors
2	Sacral	Orange	Creativity/Purpose	Use your intuition and natural skills	5: REIMAGINE Clarify and Focus	Tarot Cards, Colors, Crystals, and Elements
1	Root	Red	Practicality/Safety	Ground and embody	2: RELEASE Clear and Allow	Power Animal

Below is an example of how the reference pages will appear in each step to see how the mystical information will be presented.

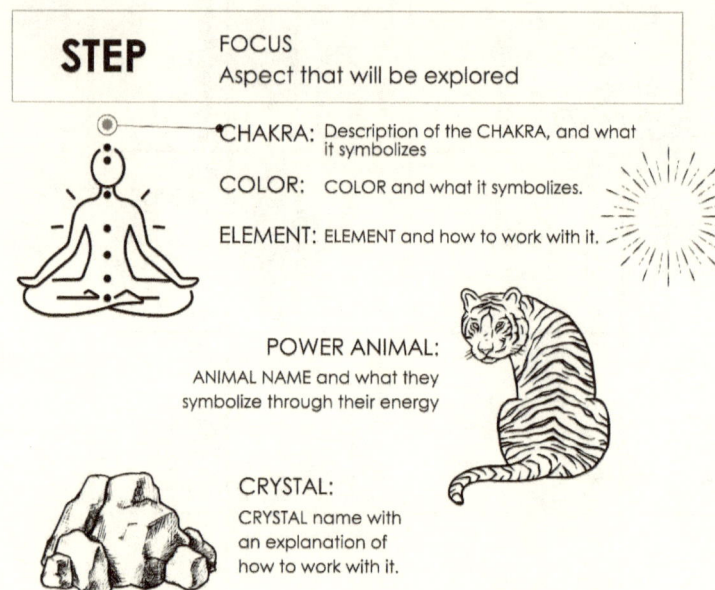

STEP FOCUS
Aspect that will be explored

CHAKRA: Description of the CHAKRA, and what it symbolizes

COLOR: COLOR and what it symbolizes.

ELEMENT: ELEMENT and how to work with it.

POWER ANIMAL:
ANIMAL NAME and what they symbolize through their energy

CRYSTAL:
CRYSTAL name with an explanation of how to work with it.

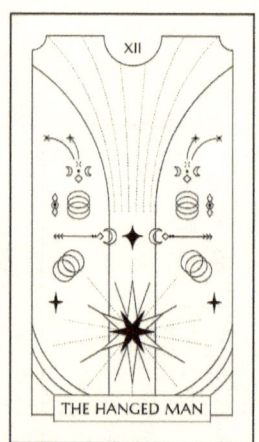

TAROT CARD:

THE HANGED MAN tarot card reflects being in the present moment. It invites you to explore how and what you might need to surrender to get a fresh perspective. While you may not know where to begin, can you remain centered in yourself through uncertainty and believe that things will unfold for your highest purpose?

XII

THE HANGED MAN

AFFIRMATION:
"'I AM' statement to inspire you."

More examples of how to work with these steps and elements are provided below. Don't be surprised if the Authentic Alchemy Path facilitates personal healing as you address different aspects of yourself and come into greater alignment.

Colors

Colors are light wavelengths representing different frequencies which are perceived by the human eye. Each color correlates with and enhances the different chakras to support health and functioning. Connecting with colors can help you better visualize the opportunities and challenges of each step and its relevant chakra. You may choose to work with or add the color related to the chakra you are working on to influence aspects of your life that may be blocked (through clothing, foods, crystals, visualization or furnishings) to create more ease and flow.

For example, working through Step 2: RELEASE will be connected to the root chakra and the color red. If you felt ungrounded when doing some of these activities, you might incorporate red into your life. Eat red foods, wear red clothing or jewelry, or add red to your surroundings to strengthen this energy and create subtle shifts.

Yellow reminded me of a childhood wall color I disliked, so the color had negative associations for me. Meanwhile, yellow is connected to the solar plexus, an area heavily correlated with personal power that can often get activated. In strengthening my solar plexus, I appreciate yellow more and use it to help support this part of the body, often working with yellow crystals to enhance this energy (see more on this below).

Crystals

Consider becoming a rock star! Stones and crystals embody powerful earth and mountain energies that have been honored throughout history and cultures for their beauty and power. Their frequencies can support you in many ways; in addition to being visually appealing, they can help ground your body or a space. Energetically, crystals create resonance, releasing or discharging energy to shift a room or a person's vibration. Crystals are powerful resources used in lasers and radio signal transmissions, underlying many aspects of technology we take for granted.

What started as an interest became a hobby and is now a passion. Crystals and rocks have become companions and tools for my meditations and personal practices, offering powerful support in my energy medicine work with clients.

Intuitively chosen crystals have been recommended for each step in the Authentic Alchemy Path, though you may select your own, either based on the chakra colors or your personal preferences, to support your growth and healing. Following the above examples, a garnet or carnelian (red) stone can provide grounding to support the root chakra (Step 2: RELEASE), while holding or meditating with citrine or amber (yellow crystals and resins) can strengthen the solar plexus to help you trust your gut (Step 6: REVEAL).

Choose whichever crystals or rocks speak to you and trust your intuition. Clear quartz, for instance, is a master healing crystal that can take on whatever energy you wish and will amplify whatever you focus on. Many of us appreciate rose quartz, which represents love and can support the heart. Consider using your favorite crystal as a touchstone throughout your journey. Learn more as you explore the first ritual in the next chapter.

Elements

We are deeply connected to the Earth and the building blocks of our civilization, as are many Indigenous communities and philosophical traditions. Working with the elements has become an intrinsic part of my personal practice. This guidebook references five primary elements: earth (grounding and composting), water (creativity and flow), air (spaciousness and possibility), fire (destruction and transformation), and ether (connection to spirit) to represent different energies you may bring into your process.

These most closely correlate to the Mayan cosmovision and the Peruvian Q'ero shamanic traditions which have influenced me the most. Different cultures emphasize other elements; for instance, traditional Chinese medicine incorporates metal and wood, while Ayurveda focuses on fire, earth and air, both systems I have also worked with. Consider which elements are most meaningful for your experience and choose whatever approach you prefer.

The elements may be used symbolically in rituals for different energies. For instance, fire is intense, strong energy that can be used to light things up or burn away old beliefs. To release something quickly and create massive change, use fire in a ritual, such as lighting a candle or creating a bonfire (like the one I used to burn old papers and release the past).

Water is fluid and changing, representing movement, creativity, flow, and healing. It can be deeply cleansing and soothing, as anyone who loves swimming or going to the beach will experience. Earth is deeply rooted and grounded, which could be used to bury something or plant new seeds. While air can feel lighter, wind is also very powerful, so you could throw something symbolic into the air (like salt or another spice) to spread it far and wide or connect with spaciousness through conscious awareness of your breath.

As you can see, choosing an element is a creative act based on what you are intuitively drawn to and depending on what you wish to strengthen or let go of to deepen your connection to the natural world. I typically ask clients to see what they feel connected to, and most intuitively know. Here are two examples of how clients have worked with water, which can be particularly cleansing and supportive and assist with healing.

After our session, Samantha, who lived near and loved the beach, was immediately drawn to water. After we had processed her experiences together, she decided to go to the beach near her home and continue our release work to forgive herself, let go of past concerns that she was ready to leave behind, and find more peace by throwing stones in the water.

David had been working through relationship challenges and holding on to a lot of pain and sadness. Following our session, he was drawn to submerge himself in the ocean, then float to be held and feel lighter. He shared that being in the water allowed him to process his grief and release pain he didn't even realize he had. Shortly thereafter, he left the city to move closer to the ocean that he loved.

Affirmations

Our words hold immense power to impact our experiences. Affirmations are positive statements of intention. Throughout this process, notice your language and word choices to communicate or describe yourself. Do you say what you really think and feel, or do you say what you believe others want to hear? Are you hesitant to speak up at all?

To become more authentic, carefully consider your language and word choices to choose messages that reinforce the desired outcome you wish to create. Rather than saying, "I don't want XYZ any longer" (a negative perspective), consider communicating, "I'm excited to be exploring new professional growth opportunities." Regularly remind yourself of this message when speaking to yourself and when sharing with others.

Focus on positivity and possibility as much as you can, over negativity and limitation. See how this changes your reality. The way you talk to yourself, and others, will directly influence how you feel about yourself, how others respond to you, and the overall quality of your interactions.

We can often be so critical of ourselves, creating constant pressure to do more. I developed a reminder for that—"I am loving, gentle, and kind with myself and with others"—to help me reset and stop internal criticism. We can use the affirmations to retrain our brains until we start to believe them and begin shifting our consciousness.

Communication goes beyond words alone. Research on nonverbal communication by Albert Mehrabian and others shows that we intuitively interpret what, how, and why someone is speaking to us to assess their integrity. On a visceral level, we notice people's body language and emotions (their energy and tone) and how they make us feel (intentions) more than what they say (their words). We perceive communication that is aligned and in sync to be authentic and have integrity.

Using positive affirmations is an inspired and motivating way to change core beliefs and shift critical internal messages and energy. Each step of the Authentic Alchemy Path offers affirmation statements to orient you to that chapter's lesson, so you will find these with the mythical inspiration references. These suggestions are starting points so you can find what works for you. You may use the affirmations provided or customize them for your needs to reframe your thinking and whatever messages you need to hear.

The most effective way to work with affirmations is to state them in positive language using active verbs from your perspective (for example: "I pursue my life path with enthusiasm and optimism," or: "My experiences empower me to find work I love"). Create new statements to rewire old, unhelpful, or critical messaging, especially when you doubt yourself or diminish your capabilities. These can be aspirational (something you hope to move toward) or reflect already existing elements of your experience that you wish to remind yourself of for encouragement and inspiration.

Reinforce your new beliefs by repeating them regularly. Consider saying your affirmations daily or whenever you notice an unproductive way of thinking. Writing them down and placing them where you can see them, for instance displayed on your desk or work area, can serve as a reminder to approach your path with positivity. Written or digital sticky notes can be left on your mirror or computer monitor where you will see them regularly.

Consider adding a physical posture or movement to reinforce the new energy in your body. Combining your words with actions creates even more powerful resonance. You're probably familiar with the expressions, "Fake it until you make it," and "Put a smile on your face." These are both examples of how we can use our body movements to support shifts in our mindset. Words are powerful, while incorporating movements kicks things up a notch. Amy Cuddy's powerful TED Talk on power poses shows how body language can energize our thinking.

Embodying positivity and what we wish to create helps to shift, integrate, and align who we can become. Tailor and update your affirmations as your needs change over time. Keep them light and playful, or punchy and energetic. Remember that shorter is better.

Tarot

Tarot is an ancient mystical tradition and form of cartomancy used for insight and divination that relies upon imagery and archetypes to uncover deeper hidden meanings and connections. The earliest tarot cards appeared in Western Europe in the 1400s, and other divination and symbolic tools have been used across diverse ancient cultures (from Egypt to Mayan glyphs, to tasseography for reading leftover tea leaves and geomancy for reading stones).

The traditional seventy-eight tarot card deck has two primary sections: twenty-two major arcana cards which represent archetypal energies, experiences, and lessons in life; and fifty-six minor arcana cards (these more closely correlate to a traditional playing card deck). "Arcana" means "mysterious or specialized knowledge, language, or information accessible or possessed only by the initiate" (according to the Merriam-Webster online dictionary) and implies secrets.

The tarot's history and varying symbolic references (from numerology to astrology and Kabbalah) are robust, lending itself to many layers of deeper meaning. Here, the focus is primarily on the relevance of certain primary archetypes that represent one's journey through life. I intuitively selected several major arcana archetypes to illuminate the lessons faced at different stages of the Authentic Alchemy Path. Brief explanations of the cards that were chosen for each step, and what they mean, can be found in the mystical reference section.

Tarot and oracle cards can be used to clarify challenges or offer insight into questions through visually or intuitively interpreting the cards and reflecting on their imagery, underlying energies, and motivations. No cards are inherently good or bad, though some traditional card names and images use words with implied judgments (like Death, the Fool, or the Devil). The tarot can offer additional inspiration and guidance to represent archetypal challenges faced in undertaking one's path to purpose placed in the context of universal challenges.

While the iconic Rider Waite Smith (RWS) deck comes from a distinct period and uses more traditional gender roles and theatrical compositions, newer decks offer different imagery and energy with hundreds of variations and unique interpretations. The minimalist-style design presented here offers a jumping-off point for your intuitive understanding of each theme. You may prefer to use your own tarot deck for imagery that speaks to you, to gain additional insights around your soul path, and how these lessons show up in your process.

For example, the Hanged Man, which appears in the sample reference page above and in Step 0: CLEAR, can be a challenging card to consider. The RWS deck shows a man hanging upside down from a tree by one leg that is bound by a rope, both hands behind his back and a golden halo around his head, like an upside-down yoga pose. He's suspended in the air yet seems serene, so there's a sense of his waiting patiently for inspiration to strike or something to happen. This card implies surrender, which is needed when pursuing a new path—letting go of the past while one is held still by time waiting for the future to unfold.

While the image included here is more abstract, there's an energy pointing downward, with multiple circles and stars on either side indicating this sense of possibility, like suspended animation before a change is ready to emerge. The invitation presented is to find your center despite the uncertainty and not knowing what may occur in the future. The Hanged Man image could be used for meditation and reflection, or simply as an invitation to get a fresh perspective on your life like you would if you were hanging upside down.

Whether you use or understand tarot cards or not, placing your journey in the context of a more mythical undertaking can be a powerful reframe of your growth process. Seeing and considering your personal evolution through the archetypal hero/heroine's journey can help you recognize that everyone faces challenges they must overcome at different points in their life. Knowing you are not alone, sharing a universal experience can make the difficult times less painful, since they are simply stages you will move through. Relying upon your creativity and personal development will help you navigate the challenges you face to become wiser and more self-actualized.

Power Animals

We share our planet with other living creatures. Most of us have deep connections to the animal kingdom, whether through beloved pets or favorite species that intrigue or inspire us. In my shamanic practice, and in many Indigenous traditions, animals represent different energies for guidance and wisdom. We can learn from each animal's unique strategies, resources, habits, and instincts to inform our journey.

I intuitively selected animals for each Authentic Alchemy Path step for the qualities they possess. See which animals resonate with you, or if you encounter them (through images, movies, dreams, or stories) in your life to remind you about what you are working on.

You may choose to connect exclusively with one animal that has a special meaning for you, or you may have different ones accompany your process. Notice if you hear a wise owl during the REALIZE step or see an eagle or hawk flying overhead in the REAP step. What does each animal symbolize for you? Explore what might need to shift within you as you move between steps, and how new energies and inspirations can support you.

Choose Your Own Adventure

Remember that this is your journey, with each step a decision point to choose how to act, feel, and approach your situation. In choosing to create a more fulfilling life, see the value of your struggle and discovery process. You are a warrior and the hero/heroine of your own life, undertaking a mythical journey.

These tools are meant to be fun and playful inspirations to get you out of your head and prompt you to consider a new perspective. Your path is less about what you do and more about moving forward, trying new things, and learning from every experience. When you feel unsure what to do next, consider these unexpected allies for guidance to remind you that you are not alone. You are always supported. You are here to do great things. In embarking on your path, may this guide offer you a companion, mentor, inspiration, and motivation.

PREPARATION

CLEAR

INTEND and PREPARE
Create a clean slate to intentionally start your process.

CHAKRA: Focus on your SOUL STAR, just above your head, to connect with your higher consciousness.

COLOR: WHITE supports you to begin your journey from a place of light and purity.

ELEMENT: ETHER brings higher consciousness and expansion to divinely guide your path.

POWER ANIMAL:
POLAR BEAR is a messenger of change bringing strength, surrender and patience.

CRYSTALS:

MOONSTONE is an inherently calming and soothing stone that can activate dreaming, clearing and release.

SELENITE is a powerful cleansing stone. It is calming and healing, and can connect you to dreams and higher realms.

TAROT CARDS:

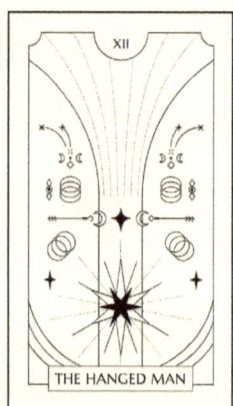

XII

THE HANGED MAN

XVII

THE STAR

THE HANGED MAN card represents being in the present moment. It invites you to explore how and what you might need to surrender to get a fresh perspective. While you may not know where to begin, can you stay centered through uncertainty and believe things will unfold for your highest purpose?

THE STAR tarot offers you optimism, inspiration, and renewal. It may be time to wish upon a star! Can you trust that the universe is guiding you and working in your favor? Believe that it will take you to wherever you are meant to be directed.

AFFIRMATION:
"I am excited to discover new possibilities."

STEP 0: CLEAR:

INTEND AND PREPARE

Alice: "Would you tell me, please,
which way I ought to go from here?"

The Cheshire Cat: "That depends a good deal
on where you want to get to."

Alice: "I don't much care where."

The Cheshire Cat: "Then it doesn't much matter
which way you go."

Alice: "... So long as I get somewhere."

The Cheshire Cat: "Oh, you're sure to do that,
if only you walk long enough."
—Lewis Carroll, *Alice in Wonderland*

- - - - - - - -

So, you are ready to discover your purpose and who you are. That can feel like a loaded, intense undertaking. The weighty responsibility and obligation to "get it right" and find what you are meant to do can seem a bit heavy and more pressure than necessary. Consider reframing your process to *discover your path and work in the world, being present for every experience that is uniquely yours.*

Of course, you may choose to wander in the desert (metaphorically speaking), take side roads, and get diverted, as I did. In fact, these detours may very well be part of your journey of becoming. Can you own and enjoy the choices you made, being okay that your life zigged when perhaps you wanted it to zag? Can you accept your direction, knowing it was an essential part of your learning? There's an opportunity to embrace the messy discovery of going through it all and being kind to yourself.

It could just be time to *stop giving a f*ck what other people think,* because it's not about anyone else but *you.*

Tell me, what is it you plan to do with your one wild and precious life?
—Mary Oliver, "The Summer Day"

As I've shared, your soul path is every experience that was meant to be part of your journey. From this perspective, each encounter serves a purpose in your life and offers you something to learn. Of course, you can be intentional and choose where to direct your energy, but don't regret the decisions you have already made which brought you to where you are now.

Many choose the path of least resistance, moving forward by default rather than by design. Reacting to what arises, then moving forward, is both convenient and expedient. While there are merits in responding to opportunities that present themselves, following wherever the river takes you can also direct you to a different destination than you would have chosen on your own. Since your journey will offer multiple possible directions to pursue, consider

how to evaluate your decisions. Can you find the best balance between wandering aimlessly and moving toward where you will find the most fulfillment?

What criteria should direct how you spend your working hours? Do you listen to and follow your heart or your head to do what you think you should? No choice is right or wrong, just different guidance. Sometimes, we pursue a job out of practicality to earn a living and pay the bills. These can be a *means* to an end, for instance to cover expenses, keep a roof over your head, and hold you over in the short term.

While a job may not be a passion project, it can create space to pursue one. Many creatives find day jobs for consistent income, benefits, and financial stability, freeing up their time to pursue their calling (making art, music, acting, healing, or building a side hustle). Addressing your financial needs is smart and practical to ensure you are in a stable place to make informed decisions for your future. Interim work can also be valuable during extended periods of under or unemployment to learn and grow while reducing financial anxiety.

A career parlays related experiences into expertise that can offer *meaning*. Building subject matter expertise and background creates the opportunity to become known in an area. The upside of branding or positioning as a specialist is being recognized for your expertise, while the downside is becoming pigeonholed, doing something you're good at but don't love.

In defining yourself by your outer profession, rather than by your personality, soul, or other wonderful inner qualities, should your career become derailed, disrupted, or upended (for instance, by a layoff, economic disruption, or other industry or structural change), you risk impacting your entire identity.

Having a calling implies a deeper connection between your work, skills, preferences, values, and vision through a greater sense of purpose and a *mission*, more than simply a means to an end; doing your work in the world based on your unique talents, life experiences, and perspectives. Having a higher purpose can feed your soul, feel like play, and bring immense pleasure and flow—that deep engagement and ease from being totally immersed in optimal experiences in the moment.

Your soul path can include all the above in your life journey to find meaning and purpose. One growth challenge that can arise is rejecting aspects of yourself to prevent you from pursuing your true purpose. Just know that avoiding your passions out of shame or being embarrassed by your gifts, through hiding, denying, or suppressing who you are won't keep you from what you are meant to do. It will find you.

Wherever you are in your journey, know that *you are on your path*. All your job experiences provide skills and lessons to inform your future choices. Jumps between jobs or work gaps were likely necessary parts of your experience. Don't regret the choices you made; simply see them as part of the journey you needed to learn from. It is more important to understand why you made those choices and translate them into meaning going forward.

Perhaps you gained incredible value cultivating a successful career until now. However, if you have been hiding your true self, calling it in to work or showing up just for the paycheck, then reconsider new work to give your life more meaning and energy.

The Authentic Alchemy Path will help you uncover and weave the many black-and-white throughlines of your various life experiences into a colorful tapestry that informs who you are and what you are here to do. Integrating and claiming your unique passions and perspectives will uncover more purpose. Your journey will reveal your world work, whether you earn a living from it or simply make time to pursue what you love in a way that nourishes and supports you.

Purpose and Passion

Your work in the world gives you purpose; it is what you are uniquely meant to do. Start by pursuing your interests to find those issues and areas that light you up and inspire you. Your purpose and passion together enable you to make a meaningful contribution, the larger impact or legacy that you are here to bring. There is a wide spectrum of possibilities available to you, some of which you may not even be aware of at this point.

Your unique journey will integrate your inspired life experiences and what you are drawn to. Avoid defining yourself or measuring success by comparison to others. Discover and choose metrics that matter to you as you evaluate whether you're making progress. This is not a race, but rather a marathon—the journey of your life. Don't be in a hurry to get to the finish line without enjoying the race. Consider what you value as you start assessing your progress and how to move forward.

» **Helpful Hint:** Consider using a dedicated journal, computer document, or notepad to capture all your Authentic Alchemy Path reflections and record your journey. A separate *So, What Do You Do?* companion workbook will be available to capture your reflections. Your notes about your check-ins, practices, exercises, and reflections will become a helpful resource for you to review your progress and see your evolution over time. Also, future exercises will invite you to refer to earlier ones and notice what has changed, so it will be useful to have your responses accessible in one place.

While you can simply read and reflect on each activity in your mind, I strongly recommend writing down your thoughts. Multiple research studies have shown that writing accesses more open and creative parts of our brains. Freehand writing may also unlock unexpected intuitive insights as you are less likely to monitor yourself and can reveal what's hiding below the surface.

CHECK-IN: Where Are You Now?

Before diving into your path, let's take a pulse check of where you are right now. Reflect on the questions below to evaluate what might be emerging for you. Naming things by formalizing them and putting thoughts to words makes them more real and tangible, giving your intentions more power. Over time, you may wish to review what has changed or shifted throughout your process relative to this baseline.

- **Readiness:**
  - ¤ Are you ready to explore new possibilities for personal and professional fulfillment?
  - ¤ How much time will you allocate to this process?
  - ¤ Are you excited or nervous to discover new things?
  - ¤ What self-critical voices may want to hold you back, blame you, or shame you?
  - ¤ What decision-making process do you prefer: using your head, heart, or both?
  - ¤ Which approach do you typically follow, and why?
  - ¤ How connected are you to your intuition and instincts?
  - ¤ How do thoughts about what you *should* do factor into your choices?
  - ¤ What is your soul yearning for?
  - ¤ How do your heart and gut feel about your soul path?

- **Expectations:**
  - ¤ Name any assumptions you notice coming up, like worrying you are too old/young, overqualified/inexperienced, capable of change/stuck (fill in the blank)?
  - ¤ Can you allow these fears to not be true?
  - ¤ Are you able to question your critical inner voice to explore new thoughts?

¤ Can you set aside the need to know exactly what you want?

¤ Are you open to what might evolve, even if you can't imagine it yet?

¤ Are you willing to question how you think about yourself, your experiences, and your opportunities?

- **Priorities:**

  ¤ Where are you in your life right now? Settled/unsettled? Early, middle, or late career? Secure, but bored or unstable, and needing more security? Anything else?

  ¤ What are your top three goals for yourself? Why?

  ¤ Which is most important to you right now: finding a job, developing your career, or uncovering your calling?

  ¤ Do you believe in finding your soul path? Does this inspire you or overwhelm you?

  ¤ Have you considered what your personal mission or legacy might be?

  ¤ What's your vision for yourself?

  ¤ Where do you want to be in the future (three to five years from now)?

  ¤ What do you hope to accomplish by next year? Within ten years?

  ¤ What would you like to get out of this guidebook process?

There are no wrong answers here. Identify where you are, so you understand your starting point. And be patient with the process. A job can, and will, evolve into a career, which can easily become a calling or personal mission. Do you appreciate your unique perspective, and can you not worry about making others happy? Consider whether you are ready to pursue more of what you truly love to create the life you want to live.

Let the natural world inspire you. Consider spirals, sacred geometric figures that continuously circle around and back, as one way of viewing your journey. Our life's work is rarely a straight line, but often follows a circular path of returning to old interests or facing seemingly similar challenges in new ways. You may revisit aspects of yourself or your work by engaging at a different level this time, perhaps with the advantage of more experience and perspective. It's not uncommon to develop a level of mastery over time, or to rediscover a renewed interest in something you previously set aside. Recognizing that life moves in cycles acknowledges continuous growth and can be liberating.

Preparing for Change

While we will explore doing inner work and responding to our circumstances, we cannot overlook how our environment directly impacts us physically, psychologically, emotionally, and energetically. Before going within (which starts with Step 1: REALIZE), let's examine how your outer environment is set up to support you. For instance, some people can't concentrate with external noise in the background, while others can't focus without music. Recognizing your individual needs will help you create and find the spaces and places that best support how you want to live and work.

My perspective on change has been influenced by training in modern feng shui. Feng shui roughly translates as "wind" and "water," and involves arranging and placing objects in spaces to create harmony and energetic flow, connecting us with the natural world and our surroundings.

As above, so below.
—Ancient Hermetic expression

Our inner and outer experiences often mirror each other. Taken literally, our external surroundings can show us what is happening within our internal landscapes. For example, stuff piled on a desk or in a closet can represent avoidance or not dealing with something,

like paying bills or holding on to things (or an old identity) that no longer fits. An empty space without artwork and devoid of personal identity can indicate an inability to commit, choose a focus, or settle down.

Let's see how your outer space might be echoing your internal emotional experience to give you some clues about where you are. While distinguishing the symptoms from the cause can be challenging, let's tackle both. Creating a fresh start begins with preparing to shed aspects of your past that are no longer needed. Are things that previously defined you still important, or are they inadvertently constricting you?

Many mythological stories use shedding old clothing to symbolize changes in identity. Similarly, you are going through a disrobing process, removing old outfits and styles that no longer fit. You may decide to discard valuable things that got damaged, or that you no longer enjoy. You could also choose to repair, upcycle, donate, or recycle things you no longer want or need to keep carrying. Maybe you realize that you will repurpose things you love but haven't used in a while, to rekindle an old interest. Consider what may be taking up space and blocking you from what you want now or what might be calling you to revisit it.

We will also look at your inner self (your beliefs, stories, behaviors, and patterns), but our initial focus is your immediate environment. In reviewing your physical space, also consider activities and how you spend your time, since these are the outer expressions of where you direct your energy now. Are previous commitments no longer bringing you meaning or joy? What activities are driven by a sense of obligation rather than by choice?

Working from the Outside In

For some people, changing their physical space is a more direct path to greater awareness than internal reflection. Through empowered space and individual clearing sessions, I help clients evaluate how to create more supportive environments that can facilitate change. Shifting our spaces brings in different energies and creates a sense of new possibilities.

CLIENT STORY: Supportive Sanctuary

My client Jane was the mother of two adolescents and two cats. She was an experienced sales professional who had worked successfully for many years at the same technology company. During COVID, she had moved with her family into a new house, obtained additional training, and was feeling ready to pursue a new professional direction, possibly starting a side hustle, and showing up in new ways. Together, we reviewed her in-home office to see how her environment could support her transition.

Her vision was for a relaxing self-care retreat where she could close the door for privacy, energetically recharge, and meditate; a cocoon for her to come back into balance. Initially assessing the space, we looked at what Jane liked most. She had collected some lovely artwork and had many cherished personal and family mementos. However, she was also tolerating things that she didn't like; for instance, an uncomfortable upholstered chair acquired at a secondhand store that had become a cluttered space where stuff accumulated. There were also objects piled up directly opposite the front door that didn't belong there, and purely functional items that didn't mean much to her personally.

Jane's desk faced a large wall with her back to a window. We decided to turn the desk around to change her view

and give her a new perspective. She brought in a beautiful, colorful rug she hadn't been using to brighten up the whole space, and she incorporated more colors, plants, crystals, and other items she loved. She also moved the side chair by the front door, covering it with a blue blanket to use for meditation. Jane also tackled her closet, clearing it out and putting in shelves to organize her things instead of piling them on top of each other.

Throughout this reorganizing process, Jane became aware of how she had previously segmented parts of her life, as had been reflected in her office's old haphazard design. Within three hours, she had transformed her space, making subtle physical adjustments using her existing resources. She could feel the shift from her intentional choices, and she felt inspired.

Jane had created a holistic, balanced, and supportive space for her growth. It reflected what she cared about and how she wanted to feel going forward. She felt a renewed sense of possibility to bring more creativity and joy into her life, and she was excited for her future.

Just as our gardens need the right land and conditions, or terroir, to grow, so do our home and work situations. Is your ground parched and thirsty, or waterlogged and needing more irrigation? Should you cut your grass, or dig up weeds? Do you have enough natural sunlight and the best location for your plants to grow? Let's consider how these gardening questions relate to your space.

EXERCISE: Consciously Clear What You No Longer Need

**Let go of the idea of who you were
(or thought you should be) to step into who
you really are and are meant to be.**
—Lenore Kantor

Growth requires space. A full cup of water will overflow if more liquid is poured in. You, too, must create some available room in your vessel (yourself and your environment) for new things to enter. Set aside as much time as necessary to work through the following areas of your physical and energetic surroundings to let go of what you no longer need.

I realize, if you intended to declutter, you might have bought a Marie Kondo book. Conscious clearing here is about making intentional choices and a commitment to what you want to create. Approach your process with a beginner's mind, openness, and willingness to take a leap of faith.

By clearing out the old to let in the new—literally, physically, and energetically—you will feel and be ready to embark on this journey with excitement. If you and your space are full or filled up (for instance, your schedule, time, and predefined beliefs), then it will be hard to let new things in. Should the thought of this exercise be completely overwhelming, commit to removing one thing (at a minimum) that you don't like and discarding or donating it to start shifting your energy.

Going from Closed to Open

Consider the two images on the chart below. There's a full circle on the left without space to add anything, and an open, empty circle on the right with space for new possibilities. Notice which one intuitively calls you. Full or empty? Closed or open? Be curious

about how it feels to consider the empty circle or blank slate. Do you have any reactions? Does it make you think of nothingness or loss (possibly negative connotations), or a fresh start (exciting possibility)? This will provide some important clues about your state of mind and willingness to embark on the change process.

GOING FROM CLOSED TO OPEN

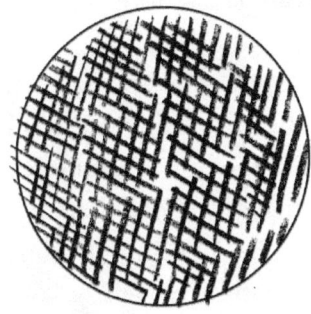
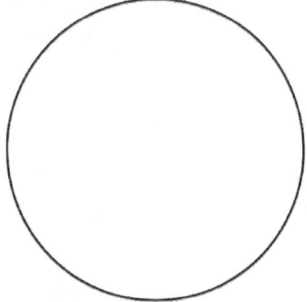

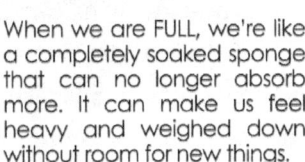

When we are FULL, we're like a completely soaked sponge that can no longer absorb more. It can make us feel heavy and weighed down without room for new things.

When we are EMPTY, we have lots of spaciousness to grow, expand and add new things. This can feel light, airy and give us a new perspective to see what might be possible.

Be aware of any resistance and be gentle with yourself to recognize how our cultural conditioning can come into play. We often place a premium on being busy. Having a "full" life might be something we enjoy or aspire to, so we fill our time and schedule with activities. Constant juggling and running nonstop on the hamster wheel can become a default habit, and perhaps, a part of our identity.

We can define our value by being constantly active and engaged with work, and we may not even realize how this creates drama to generate even more activity. Seemingly important activities can distract us from noticing how we really feel. Do you avoid slowing down to pause or reflect because it feels uncomfortable?

No judgment here. I relate to this pattern as a former New Yorker always on the go who used to joke about pushing old ladies walking too slowly out of the way (while only in my mind, it's still hard to admit that was part of my reality). I was always in a rush and a state of urgency, constantly "doing" because "being" felt quite uncomfortable and scary. I equated being calm or relaxed with being unproductive, a judgment clearly based on underlying beliefs around needing to prove oneself and the value of working "hard."

Reflect again on the image and consider how the full circle doesn't have room for new ideas, whereas an empty canvas is a blank page to be filled in at will. You can be intentional about what you choose to let into your space.

In what ways do your things validate you or make you feel valued? What do you find yourself holding on to? Where do you fill your space or yourself (with stuff, activities, food, or commitments ... you name it)? Retaining things, particularly those that represent achievements or accomplishments, can be meaningful, while they may also tie you down or be a way to protect yourself.

Believing that "the one who dies with the most toys wins" (attributed to millionaire Malcolm Forbes in the 1980s) illustrates our cultural bias toward accumulation. Consider an alternative, the Swedish art of death cleaning, which encourages giving away objects as one ages to unburden oneself and others from dealing with too much stuff.

May you find your happy place somewhere that feels right for you. The important thing is to consider what you have and whether it feels appropriate for where you are in your life now. Embracing a new state of being may not be easy, yet you can create the groundwork to allow new possibilities to enter.

Review the questions below from a place of inquiry and see what comes up and how you feel. What do you notice? If this feels too overwhelming to contemplate for your entire home space, focus initially on your working space.

- **ENVIRONMENT: Consider what would make your living and working spaces more productive, pleasurable, and playful.**
    - ¤ Do you have space to think, plan, and create? Have you wanted to move things around to change your layout?

¤ Has any physical clutter accumulated? What might you be avoiding dealing with? Does anything physically block, mentally or emotionally get in the way of clear thinking?

¤ Is there anything you could move out of your workspace, fix, donate, throw away, or give to someone to give you more spaciousness?

¤ Where is the clutter located? What do you notice in that space? How might you use the space differently if it were clear?

¤ Does everything in your rooms have a purpose or use (whether that's practical or emotional)? What have you been tolerating or holding on to out of guilt, obligation, or practicality that perhaps you don't need to keep or accept any longer (for instance, gifts, makeshift furniture, or items to be fixed)?

¤ Who do you want to be? Does your space reflect your true personality and preferences (choice of colors, patterns, materials, lighting, physical location)?

¤ Which things are you holding on to (consider old work materials, clothing, or past reminders you've been attached to) that you could let go of now? Are you ready to release them? If not, what do they represent for you?

¤ What would you like to have more space for (such as exercise, meditation, or other creative activities)? Is there room?

¤ Is there enough natural light in your room, or is it dark? Do you need more lamps or to paint the walls a different color?

- **EMOTIONS: Be aware of how you feel.**

  ¤ Have you been holding in any heavy feelings (such as sadness, anger, resentment, regret, relief, or frustration) that need to be released?

  ¤ What unacknowledged emotions from previous experiences may need to be expressed? Use this opportunity to acknowledge what might need to move.

¤ Do you need to cry, scream, yell, or simply have a conversation about something that's been weighing on your mind? Can you do that now?

- **TIME: Notice the commitments in your schedule.**

  ¤ What obligations must you take care of? Why? Is your initial rationale for making those commitments still valid?

  ¤ How are you choosing to spend your free time? Do you engage in enjoyable activities, or simply try to recover from your day?

  ¤ Are you doing things that no longer fill you up as they may have in the past? How can you do meaningful activities without a sense of obligation?

  ¤ Have you blocked out time for reading this guidebook and doing the exercises?

  ¤ Do you have time available for personal reflection? If not, can you rearrange and find time for your growth? Schedule this commitment in your calendar (daily or weekly) and make it real.

- **TIMING: Explore new possibilities now.**

  ¤ How do you feel about change? Are you ready to embark on a journey of discovery?

  ¤ How stable is your work situation? Are you in a period of change (graduating from school, getting fired or laid off from work, whether by your choice or not)?

  ¤ Do you feel dissatisfied, burned-out, or unhappy with your current work, boss, or company?

  ¤ What stage of your life are you in? Are there any life changes (age, relationship situation, health, or family issues) that may be leading you to rethink your priorities?

  ¤ What is the voice of your soul telling you? Do you feel a sense of urgency around making a change now? Why?

- **ENERGY: Consider your ability to show up.**
  - ¤ How is your overall energy and enthusiasm?
  - ¤ What might need to shift for you to feel more inspired?
  - ¤ Does your space feel heavy and stuck, or light and open (or anything else)?
  - ¤ Do you notice undesirable energy in any of your rooms?
    - » You can bring in fresh energy or clear heavy spaces by opening windows, ringing bells, or lighting incense (sage, palo santo, or other natural herbs) to clear heaviness.
    - » Lighting a candle and walking around the space with the intention to clear it can also bring in new energy.
  - ¤ Do you need to ground yourself more? Can you make time in your day to go outside and be in nature?

- **PSYCHOLOGY/THOUGHTS: Connect with and acknowledge your inner knowing.**
  - ¤ How do you talk to yourself?
  - ¤ What do you think of your situation?
  - ¤ Do you like or dislike your space? Why?
  - ¤ What does your gut tell you about where you live and work?

Grab your journal and reflect on this experience or talk with a friend. What have you noticed coming up? Conscious clearing can and should be an ongoing process. Right now, the goal of this exercise is to notice your readiness to move forward.

- - - - - - - -

Creating rituals and activities to clear and release objects will symbolically support you to open to new possibilities while also helping you get into the mindset, energetic space, and physical space to let go and create change. If these reflections were challenging or overwhelming for you, what is one thing you can change? Could you select one object to represent who you have been or what you no longer want to let go of? Any act of releasing the old will confirm your desire to step forward into the new.

<u>RITUAL:</u> Teacher Stone Talisman

You can approach your new path to purpose with joy and excitement, or with fear and trepidation. Your process can be playful, fun, and inspiring instead of stressful or overwhelming. Having allies to support you can help; enter your personal talisman, or teacher stone.

Did a favorite teacher ever inspire and support you? We all benefit from mentors, guides, and advisors in our lives. We can also find inspiration from the natural world. Consider choosing or creating a talisman or magical resource to guide and support you on your journey. This can be a crystal, piece of jewelry, or some other meaningful object, such as a wooden or metal figurine, for instance. Maybe you have a four-leaf clover or lucky rabbit's foot you relate to.

When I decided to write this book, I selected a beautiful purple asterite crystal sphere to keep me divinely guided. It sat on my desk next to my computer, where I could see it daily for inspiration. I also used it to meditate with and support my focus and commitment. I loved having a visual and physical representation of my book that I could pick up in my hand to connect and engage with.

Your talisman can be an important touchstone for you throughout your process. I recommend choosing something physical that you can easily see, hold on to, or wear. While cut flowers are beautiful, they may wither and die; however, if you have a green thumb and a strong connection to caring for the natural world, then a plant could be a wonderful option.

Select any object that is inspiring and meaningful for you, but you don't need to go out and buy something for this occasion. Find

something you already have that calls you; for instance, something practical (like a key or coin) or anything that symbolizes what you desire, so seeing it will connect you to your vision.

Many of my clients feel intuitively drawn to something they've had or consider special. You will know what's right for you. It could be a photograph, postcard, miniature car, antique watch, or other personal memento, for example. Whatever speaks to you is what matters. A close friend keeps a heart-shaped stone I gave her as a reminder to connect to her heart.

Once you choose your talisman to work with, imbue it with power by infusing your intentions into it. First, you can check in and ask its permission to work with you. This can be an energetic exchange, and you will likely feel internally what is calling you to connect with it. Know this object has some wisdom or deeper meaning for you.

Tell it what you hope to accomplish on your path. Hold it, give it positive energy, talk to it, and share your dreams, desires, and goals. Let it know that you have chosen it to support you, and you would like it to bring you fulfillment and prosperity. Let it be a reminder that what you want is already on its way to you. Just as some people hold rosaries, worry stones, or mala beads to accompany their prayers, you can choose to use this in whatever way you wish.

**You are now ready to start cocreating
with the universe.**

PRACTICAL CAREER PATH APPROACHES

To help you prepare for the path ahead and consider your future, I'm sharing some options to begin thinking about so you can plan and adapt your approach accordingly. This section focuses on whether and how to prepare to do your own thing (start a business, or begin freelancing or consulting work), switch careers, and manage your expectations around the change process.

This chapter offers some suggestions for how to manage your mindset in approaching a change of direction. Why? Because having guided many people through career transitions, I've found that individuals often underestimate the challenges involved in making a significant move in a new direction. This is intended to offer some perspective, ideas, practical suggestions, and alternative approaches. With this information, you won't be blindsided ("I wish someone had told me …") because you will have been forewarned and can better prepare and anticipate what may lie ahead.

Stay, or Cut Bait

The Authentic Alchemy Path is yours to follow, whether you find more fulfilling work through traditional paths, within established roles or organizations, pursuing your current interests more deeply, or through less conventional routes that may be more creatively

inspired. Becoming an entrepreneur or starting your own business are equally viable options that have personally given me incredible freedom and satisfaction as a soulpreneur, working in alignment with my values.

You may desire freedom, flexibility, and self-determination—to break free of the rigid nine-to-five (or eight-to-six, depending on your job) grind. Not every organizational role follows those hours or traditional demands, as increasingly forward-thinking companies provide employees with more opportunities to create greater work/life balance. However, in reviewing the exercises and practices in the book, you may discover you really want or need to do your own thing.

If this sounds like you, you may already have an inkling that going out on your own in some capacity (whether working freelance for creative gigs, creating a side hustle, doing consulting and advisory work for hire, or launching a business) is something intriguing. Maybe you haven't been ready to take the leap because of family obligations, financial concerns, or just plain fear. I get it; that was me, too.

How Comfortable Are You with Risk?

My invitation, if you are considering doing your own thing, is to consider your overall risk tolerance. You can't prepare and plan enough. Starting with a side hustle (doing your preferred work outside of another paid job on weekends, evenings, or online) is an effective way to start experimenting and get experience under your belt until you feel ready to go all in on a full-time basis.

Know what you need to feel supported and confident in making the change, to minimize your stress and risk if you are concerned about financial stability. Entrepreneurship involves a high level of uncertainty, so make sure you are prepared for the emotional ups and downs as well.

Ensuring you have resources to support you (such as savings to cover an extended period of potentially lower income, health insurance, or a business support network), and planning for how to market and promote yourself (for instance, through networking and relationship building, social media, events, or other forums) will help minimize your anxiety. We will explore how to build your support team (in Step 5: REIMAGINE) and how to communicate your value (in Step 4: REFRAME).

> ## Most people overestimate what they can do in one year and underestimate what they can do in ten years.
> —Bill Gates

As with most things, the "planning fallacy" leads us to inaccurately predict how long progress will take. From my experience, the minimum amount of effort for any new initiative to start gaining traction and producing any kind of initial results is typically within three months, minimum. This is where you will start to see some initial feedback to your outreach; however, it may take significantly longer (a year or more) to create meaningful change.

Factor sufficient time into your outreach plans, and plan conservatively. Eight to twelve interactions or touch points are typically needed for any kind of customer (buyer or prospect) to move from interest to action (for instance, when converting a potential opportunity to want to buy or hire you), which means that it can take time to find your ideal audience, and for them to buy from or hire you.

At a minimum, plan for six months (and likely more) of savings to cover your expenses and hold you over and consider part-time work for additional income. Remember, there are two sides to the balance sheet: income (how much money you are earning) and expenses (how much money you are spending). If one side is steady, then consider shifting the other to create more cash flow. Reducing your costs (like limiting your lattes or moving to a less expensive place) is an effective way to gain control of your budget.

Steps 3 through 5 (RECLAIM, REFRAME, and RE-IMAGINE) cover research, messaging, and experimentation that will be particularly valuable for entrepreneurs. Through these processes, you will develop clarity and confidence to do what you want and practice in lower-stakes situations. Again, consider your comfort with uncertainty, and know your personal requirements and nonnegotiables, to figure out the best way to create your dream work.

How to Make a Career Switch

If you are unhappy with your current line of work, you may already know you want to switch your career altogether to find more purpose and meaning. Fabulous! Design your path to allow new possibilities to unfold. Release the requirement to place all your hopes in finding a specific next job or role at a given company or industry. This puts too much pressure and limitations on what could be possible, so remember to leave room for synchronicity. You can't know what you don't know yet. Allow things to unfold.

One of the biggest challenges in changing jobs or a career is convincing prospective employers you have the necessary skills for a specific role, since many seek proven experience that demonstrates you already meet their requirements. Most companies want to hire someone who has done that exact work previously. You may need to recharacterize your experience using their language to the extent possible. This doesn't mean lying or falsifying your background; rather, it's about creating a new narrative and messaging that translates your background to the skills they need. You can also start taking on projects (paid or unpaid) and/or get additional training or certifications to add more relevant expertise to your tool kit.

Making a lateral job move to do the same or similar work at a company that aligns with your values is another effective way to make a transition. This can help you figure out whether the organization or the way they operate was out of sync, and you can find a better position for your interests. It is often easier to change jobs within an existing company where you are known, rather than switching your job, company, and industry all at the same time. It can be more challenging to persuade a potential employer that you have what it takes to completely take on a job that doesn't resemble anything you've done previously.

Let's be practical; making several job switches may be required before you find your best-fit position that has everything you want.

There are several advantages to having a job. Of course, it can be helpful to generate income to support you; gainful employment of any kind is often a smart move because it will help pay the bills ("a bird in the hand is worth two in the bush"). You will also gain valuable practical work experience, even if it's not directly related to your desired employment. And, finally, you will be actively engaged, which can stave off distress and help you stay positive while you search for your ideal work.

While you may benefit more over the long run from finding work directly related to what you care most about, I believe that doing any work is better in the short term than doing no work to resource you and give you more experience. We each want to be on our path to purpose, yet sometimes, we get misdirected or need to make pit stops along the route to refuel. Only you and your circumstances can determine what makes the most sense for your personal situation.

Working full time can reduce your availability to pursue your personal interests. It's a trade-off that only you can evaluate. Many people explore new work opportunities while they are gainfully employed, and it can reduce the pressure to take the first thing that comes along. At the same time, working at something you don't love can become a distraction. Whatever you choose, be intentional.

It can be helpful to stay in a given job for a year or more if you have limited previous experience or have jumped around a lot without prior stable employment. Again, be practical. If you started a job that wasn't exactly what you wanted, then shortly thereafter found a more ideal role, you could still move to the new position with the goal of making a longer-term commitment.

For those with financial flexibility, unpaid opportunities (such as volunteering, internships, or interim projects) are another way to gain skills. This is one way to explore different creative pursuits if you can afford time away from paid work. All experiences are valuable, even those that reveal what we don't like, which just help us redirect and clarify what we desire.

Regardless, the *stepping-stone approach* requires a longer-term view as you make changes to build skills, gain experience, and increase your confidence and credibility over time before landing where you really want. Committing to your vision, developing your knowledge, and building expertise will help you learn and position yourself better, even though it may take several roles and more time before you land in your optimal position.

A complete career change is possible with focus, commitment, and persuasion. This requires playing the long game, knowing that it may take you several years and work experience to transition into your ideal work. Persistence and positivity are required to stay motivated. As you work through the Authentic Alchemy Path, the more clarity you have around how to *REFRAME* your experience (Step 4) and *REIMAGINE* your work (Step 5), the more effective you will be in pivoting.

Have a clear vision, be confident in your abilities, connect to others in your chosen area, and learn to effectively communicate your contribution and impact. Beyond knowing what you want, getting hired by others requires convincing them you are the best person for what they need. Focus on demonstrating why and how you add value to any organization or potential customers. Prepare and clarify your positioning through the book's exercises to develop your knowledge, mastery, and unique angle to leapfrog into something completely new.

The guide's practices will help you explore what interests you and clarify what you love. Build experience through practical experiments to increase your knowledge and understanding. Research, on-the-job training, and/or hands-on experience gained through coursework, projects, or volunteering will help you learn more, do the work, and enhance your credibility.

Minimize Expectations to Make Room for Possibility

Consider rethinking any expectations about what "should" happen by a specific date. This can create hidden pressure (for you, others, and your work) and set you up for disappointment. Pursuing perfection, or trying to meet unrealistic deadlines, can create unnecessary stress. This process is not about having regrets for achieving anything less than exactly what you want. It's about enjoying your path and learning from every experience along the way. You don't need to compromise your vision, though being practical and recognizing where you are and what you need most at this moment is helpful.

Seek your own balance between being practical and achieving your vision, recognizing that time frames may be unpredictable. Also, don't dismiss unexpected opportunities or risk limiting your options. You can't know where something might lead. And recognize that no one owes you anything, so you can't predict what the future will bring.

Fulfilling work comes from the best alignment of your skills, preferences, and values, and finding the people and places that appreciate what you bring. Pursue your best work opportunities by considering which strategies will most support your process, whether it's through interim roles or other opportunities that give

you more skills. Find ways to leverage every experience to move you toward your goals and live in alignment with your broader values and life purpose.

How Long to Strike Gold and Find Your Soul Purpose?

Before starting this journey, you may wonder how long it will take to find your way and "land" in your ideal situation. My crystal ball is in the shop, so I'm going to be honest with you and say I just can't tell you. Sorry. There is no end game destination on this path, just you and your own timeline and ambition.

I could recommend eight weeks to complete the guide's eight-step journey, but a chapter a week may not be enough time for you to find your ideal work. I also can't know where you are now in your process, or how long it will take you to complete the exercises and reflections and gain experience. I've seen super-ambitious and driven MBA students decide what they want, clearly articulate their focus, and find new roles quickly (within several months), while others struggle to uncover their direction and find their right work (taking two years or more).

Tom, a senior technology executive, reached out to me after leaving a new job he had been in for less than a year. He no longer enjoyed the work he was known for and wanted to make a change after being unhappy in his last few jobs. At the same time, he was anxious about being unemployed and knew he needed to work immediately to stay busy and relevant.

Tom's determination and initiative landed him in a new corporate executive role within three months, uncommon *to secure a senior position so quickly. Typically, those with extensive experience undergo much longer job searches (potentially two years or more) to meet their highly specialized skill sets and requirements.*

Even though Tom had wanted to pivot significantly and redirect his career to a completely different industry and role that interested him, he returned to the exact work he wanted to leave, because that's where his experience, connections, and credibility lay. He continued in related positions for six more years, eventually transitioning to a similar role, but in a different industry that was more aligned with his ambitions. I never found out if he regretted staying in the same roles for so long, but it seemed to be the right choice for him at the time.

It can be easy to take what comes your way. Sometimes, it's the right thing to do; other times, defaulting to something practical can be a trap, a way to avoid doing the work needed to understand yourself better and pursue your true longing. You may ultimately compromise what you want by extending your process if you avoid doing the inner work.

Finding an ideal path that combines all your desires can take time. You might realistically plan for six months at a minimum, or a year or longer if you are making a significant change. That way, you can manage your expectations rather than expecting to find something in a month, only to get completely caught off guard. Decide what matters most to you—working in the perfect job, or earning a living until you find the best opportunity. Once you know what to prioritize, you can act accordingly. Your patience may be rewarded, and you may also need to stay positive and manage your mindset while you wait.

How to Find Your Soul's Calling

Finding your soul path is akin to searching for a soulmate. Do you believe there's only one ideal match made in heaven for you, or might different people suit you depending on your life stage? A soulmate could be a best friend forever (BFF), partner, spouse, lover, or twin flame who shares all your passions, and you might have multiples. Some relationships are meant for a lifetime, while others are for a specific purpose or time. Finding your path is your unique soul's journey.

Your life may have a purpose you can't fully appreciate. Every experience, even if it didn't make sense at the time, gave you some knowledge, wisdom, or skill that informed your life. Your path is integrating all these experiences into a whole.

How will you choose to interpret and integrate those experiences to infuse them with meaning? Consider weaving a beautiful tapestry from all the threads of your unique interests. Recognize what makes you special, own your talents, and know that no one else has exactly the background that you have accrued over your lifetime. Having your dreams and experiences intermingle and evolve organically with patience and persistence will allow it all to unfold.

Acknowledge, then ignore the critical voice telling you what you should or shouldn't do. That internal critic is trying to protect you from taking a risk, making a change, putting yourself out there, and getting hurt or rejected or being more successful than others in your family. Maybe some previous bad experiences taught you to stay small, to not share yourself, or to suppress your desires because it didn't feel safe. So many reasons and excuses can stop us from finding the fulfillment we desire, and we need to recognize and dismiss them.

Self-criticism and doubt are destructive and unhelpful. Notice your negative Nancy or Nick as fear. Hearing the message, "No, don't do that!" is a powerful clue pointing out where you really want to go but are likely too afraid to. Get underneath the surface, and discover what your inner voice and soul want before trying to deny it. Uncover these fears to pursue your purpose.

PRACTICE: Set Your Intention and Imagine What You Want

You picked up this guidebook to find yourself and presumably create positive change in your life. How can you realize what you want to manifest and make it real? Commit to making intentional and authentic choices about your future going forward.

Give yourself permission to have what you want with curiosity and openness. Acknowledging and stating your desires makes them more tangible. Your openness signals readiness for something new and allows others to start responding. So, are you ready to look at what you want?

What do you hope to get from this process, and what is your deepest desire? How can you make it yours? Our actions follow our visions and beliefs. Let's begin with the ends in mind to start imagining the garden we want to create.

What does your garden look like? Is it wild and untamed, like a field of wildflowers; or is it slightly contained, yet still creative and filled with whimsy, like a British garden? Or, would you prefer to build a beautiful, structured garden with paved pathways and boxwood hedges, like a French *jardin*? Take a moment to consider exactly what your ideal life and work could look like. Let yourself imagine all that you desire. Now, set the intention that you are ready to make it happen. Even if you don't know how just yet, you are ready to start the process.

PHASE 1:
INNER WORK

REALIZE

DISCOVER and SEE
Continue your INNER WORK.
Explore where you are now and what you want to create.

CHAKRA: Activate your THIRD-EYE chakra to connect to your vision

COLOR: INDIGO BLUE to connect with your intuition.

ELEMENT: AIR encourages lightness, expansion, and openness to possibility.

POWER ANIMAL:
Connect with OWL to expand your intuitive awareness, trust your inner wisdom and knowing.

CRYSTALS:

LABRADORITE is a deeply mystical stone that can help you navigate change and trust yourself.

SODALITE encourages finding positivity, truth and connecting with your intuition.

TAROT CARD:

Reflect on THE DEVIL tarot card to consider any unhelpful attachments, habits or vices that may be holding you back from having what you desire and where you want to create new relationships.

AFFIRMATION:

"I see with real eyes, no more lies, what is true."

STEP 1: REALIZE

DISCOVER AND SEE (PART 1)

Where Are You Now?

To make smart, thoughtful decisions about your future, you must recognize your present experience with honesty and awareness. By seeing what is working (or not working), you can then assess what you might need to change to create more happiness and fulfillment. Do you know what you desire, or do you realize you need a shift but are unsure how to move forward? Sometimes, imagining a new and different reality can be difficult. We must understand where we are to properly orient ourselves to what comes next.

We will explore why you want what you want, to help you get clear on your own motivations and avoid comparison and/or competition (looking at others to determine your choices). The fear of missing out (FOMO) is a pervasive aspect of our culture that places happiness just outside our reach, and it is the cause of so much striving and pushing without questioning why.

Understanding where your desires come from helps you start to create your own experience. Reality-testing by asking questions, gathering information, and gaining real experiences will help you clarify what you want. This will help you avoid the disappointment of not having what you want, or worse, getting it only to discover it's not what you expected after all.

Just because you want something, doesn't mean you can or are meant to have it. Misalignment can happen due to bad luck, poor timing, and external factors beyond your control. Agency comes from realizing which choices are within your control and which are not. Later chapters will explore how to manage things beyond your control and how to balance or adjust expectations.

Can you separate your dreams (what you think you want) from what will truly fulfill you? Consider what is most important to you and how your vision came to be:

- Why do you want what you do?

- Where did your ideal life come from?

- What inspired your vision?

- Who do you know who does that work or has that life?

Reflecting on the various influences on your life (family, friends, media, community) can help you better understand which drivers are motivating you. Are they coming from within or without?

Ways to Get Stuck

Many individuals struggle to find their path, make little progress with searching for new opportunities, or are unable to choose a direction and communicate their goals. They wonder why they can't build momentum and why they have difficulty positioning and presenting themselves effectively (for instance, through their résumé, on their LinkedIn profile, or even in conversations). This happens for various reasons. They may not understand the job requirements, or they're pursuing what they think they *should* want, not what they really want. Different causes, similar outcomes. They may not trust that they have what it takes to pursue their true passion, so they start to explore other options. They compromise, settle, or become ambivalent and can't focus.

So, what happens? Not much. They don't make progress, and they feel frustrated, anxious, and overwhelmed.

Why can't they move forward? They haven't done enough inner work to know themselves or validate what they would really enjoy doing by gathering information through outer work. They don't know what is needed to get where they want from where they are now, and they haven't made the commitment to understand what's involved. Do they have the required skills or certifications? Do they need more experience? Are they interested in the work the job involves? They don't know what they don't know, and then they blame themselves or keep treading water.

Perhaps you can relate to this experience. If so, do not fret, because the following exercises will help you move through confusion to find more clarity, build your confidence, and communicate your value. This doesn't happen overnight, but engaging in the process will help you find more focus.

Exciting jobs or roles with big titles can sound great and important, until you realize what the work entails. Do you enjoy administrative activities like filing reports, developing budgets, managing conflicts, giving feedback, working on teams, or pushing through organizational politics and BS to get sh*t done? Many managerial roles often require activities like this.

Buyer beware: know what is involved in a specific role before you pursue it. Review the requirements and how they fit into your vision. Consider your big picture and recognize your specific gifts and talents to find and create the right fit for you—by understanding your truth.

Know Yourself

The Authentic Alchemy Path starts with approaching change from a place of awareness, seeing things as they really are. Knowing your current reality helps you create a road map to exciting possibilities in the future.

Do you know what makes you unique? Consider all the crazy, silly, foolish, exciting, and brilliant things you've done in your life. What ties them all together? *You!* You know things, have been places, have seen the world, and then some. You have many interesting things to share if just given the chance. I know you are here for a reason: to share and bring your insights, your own blend of special, secret sauce.

Your individual essence is that distinct constellation of attributes that includes your skills, interests, humor, background, personality, style, and preferences. As we've seen above, the more you know yourself, the easier your quest for purpose and meaning will be because you will have a clear destination. Our goal in Step 1: REALIZE is to help you answer the following questions:

- Who am I?

- What do I stand for?

- What do I want to do?

- Why do I care?

- Which work, activities, and environments do I prefer?

We will look at two important elements. First, your *FUTURE VISION* will clarify where you want to be. Here you will explore:

- What you want to create (your vision)

- What you care about (your values)

- What you're good at (your strengths)

- Who you enjoy being with (your community)

- How you like to work (your ideal culture)

Then, we will consider your *CURRENT SITUATION* to understand where you are now. This will help you to uncover the disconnects in your experience—any feelings of unhappiness, disappointment, or frustration.

This chapter focuses on your future vision and where you are now, while the next chapter, Step 2: RELEASE, will help you understand what may be blocking you and what is getting in your way so you can address those issues and move forward. Here, you will uncover your *PAST GAP,* those areas that hold you back:

- Where you struggle (your challenges)

- What's blocking you (your weaknesses)

- How you limit yourself (your attachments)

- Which thoughts diminish your confidence (your mindset)

- What unhelpful stories you tell yourself (your self-talk)

- Which habits may constrict you (your patterns)

Acknowledging the disconnects between where you are and where you want to be will help you pinpoint the sources of your unhappiness, so you can take thoughtful actions to move forward with more ease.

EXERCISE (Part 1): Life Work Assessment

Let's clarify what you want to do, and why, giving you more insight into your preferences and nonnegotiable requirements, as well as your weaknesses and dislikes. Seeing the big picture, and understanding your specific gifts and talents, makes it easier to pursue what you desire.

With your journal, get into a relaxed and meditative state with thirty minutes to an hour of undisturbed time for reflection. This exercise has four different parts, so you may decide to review them separately over time. You may want to add more thoughts later upon further reflection. Let's see what is true for you right now in your current situation.

1. YOUR VISION: WHERE DO YOU WANT TO BE? (FUTURE)

Review the questions below, and write, draw, or reflect on your responses. Imagine yourself three to five years, or even ten years, into the future (depending on your age and stage). Let's look at different aspects of your life and work.

- **You:** What do you want? Describe what you would like to have in your life (people, experiences, activities, things …). Who do you want to be? What is your life like? How would you like people to describe you? Consider three to five words you would like your friends and family to recognize about you. How do you feel? Which activities light you up? What are you making time for (health and wellness, hobbies and personal interests, relationships, spiritual or personal growth pursuits)? What brings you joy? Notice what you care about and what seems most important.

- **Your Work and Professional Situation:** What kind of work would you like to be doing (activities, possible jobs, companies, industries)? What impact would you like to make in the world?

What would you like to be known for? How do you feel about your work and contribution? Are you part of a large or small organization; private, public, or nonprofit; or are you running your own business? Which three to five words would you like people to associate with you and your work (your professional brand) when they think of you?

- **Your Lifestyle and Personal Situation:** Where would you like to live? Get into some details about the type of environment, location, amount of space, and feeling. How would you prefer to spend your time? What important priorities would you be focused on? Who are you spending time with (family, friends, community)? What does your ideal day look like?

Once you've finished capturing the picture of your ideal future life, take a few moments to reflect on how that felt. What came up for you? Were there any unexpected, interesting themes or ideas to pay attention to going forward that you may have dismissed, underestimated, or overlooked before?

We can sometimes surprise ourselves when our unconscious minds have space and time to dream, and we allow ourselves to explore what we might really enjoy. *Write down your top three takeaways from this reflection.*

2. YOUR SITUATION: WHERE ARE YOU NOW? (CURRENT)

Let's explore your life and work now, to uncover more insight. Notice any questions that are challenging to answer or where you experience resistance. Does this remind you of what you don't have, or does it bring up doubts and frustrations? This exercise will be happening on two levels. First, you will clarify what you care about. Second, you should observe how you respond to the questions and where you have strong feelings arise, which will reveal information about your experience.

Some clients have found answering these questions challenging, so I encourage them to come back to anything that they are uncertain about. You may also choose to journal on what you notice to get more insight. Take your time with this process, and don't feel you need to rush through it. More information may come through upon further reflection.

Your Personal Preferences

- **Life Stage:** Which life stage are you in now? How might this impact your needs? Twenties (growth), thirties to forties (family), fifties (preretirement), sixties-plus (retirement).

- **Time:** What does your day look like? Which activities do you spend your time on? Are you doing things you enjoy?

- **Skills/Strengths:** What are you good at? What do you relate to most naturally? If you can't think of specific strengths, find examples of things you've done that were easy and/or satisfying and had positive outcomes.

- **Preferences:** What activities do you enjoy doing? A good way to understand this is, if left to your own devices, which tasks would you naturally choose to do first?

- **Values:** What do you care about? What ideas or ways of relating are important for you to have in your life, friends, work? Try to generate your own list, but if you get stuck, two options to consider are the University of Pennsylvania's Authentic Happiness: Values in Action (VIA) Test or Brené Brown's "Dare to Lead" List of Values (further information about these is provided in the "Additional Resources" section at the back of the book).

Note: Values operate on multiple levels and often underlie many aspects of our experiences that we don't realize because they may not be explicit.

Maxine, an experienced senior executive working at a small company, and mother of two, realized how unhappy she had been in her most recent jobs but wasn't exactly sure why. The work would initially be engaging, then would become mundane or uninspiring. She was hesitant about making yet another change, assuming that all businesses would be similar.

As we explored more, we examined specific issues that frustrated Maxine the most. She realized that she enjoyed working from home and having a certain amount of autonomy; however, she became frustrated when leadership began micromanaging and second-guessing her decisions and limiting her flexibility. These experiences constricted her autonomy and creativity.

We determined she needed to find environments and managers with work styles that aligned with her values (freedom and decision-making authority). As a senior leader, high performer, and top contributor, she wanted to be trusted. In acknowledging how important these elements were to her; she had a big aha moment that she could find and choose different environments in the future.

- **Motivations:** What drives you? What impact do you want to make? This gets under the surface to explore what inspires you to act.

- **Risk Tolerance:** How comfortable are you with change, uncertainty, and growth? Are you open to not knowing how the future might unfold, or do you prefer to control as much as possible? Make choices that align with your overall comfort level on the risk/reward spectrum. For instance, larger established organizations are often more stable than emerging, high-growth startups or starting your own business. Certain business sectors are more easily impacted by economic disruptions than others, even for established companies. Do you thrive on challenge and want to carve your own path, or do you prefer consistency and stability? Consider your threshold and tolerance for ambiguity, and choose accordingly, seeking situations that match your comfort level.

- **Focus:** Where and which activities do you direct your attention to when you work? On a spectrum of preferring breadth versus depth, where do you fit? Neither style is better or worse, though we often prefer one or the other, which can be helpful to understand. Generalists tend to be good at many things and enjoy variety, though they can also develop expertise in specific industries or functional verticals, whereas specialists prefer to focus on developing in-depth knowledge of particular functions or areas.

  - ¤ **Generalist:** Do you prefer gaining a broad understanding of a subject at a high level? Do you consider yourself more of a jack-of-all-trades (and potentially a master of none), able to jump in and get things done with little direction, likely able to adapt to changing requirements, and adept at working with more ambiguity? Can you describe the types of activities you find most interesting?

  - ¤ **Specialist:** Do you tend to dig deep, uncovering details and fine points, particularly around topics that you are interested in? Would you choose to become a subject matter expert in a focused area? What are you most interested in?

- **Background:** What is your work experience? Include any paid, part-time, freelance, project-based, consulting, or volunteer work you have done after high school or since college.

  - ¤ List the various jobs or roles you've had, any titles or job functions, and dates. You may also include hobbies and interests outside of traditional work, if you have specific passions (like travel missions or sports activities). Capture a few quick bullet points about which aspects of each job you enjoyed or excelled at. Don't worry if you've done a lot of different things. This is natural for individuals with multiple passions, or those who fell into their work by luck or circumstance.

Note: This information will be helpful if you need to develop your résumé and wish to do it concurrently with this process. Capture this information in a document that you can update and expand upon when you have clarified your messaging.

- **Trends:** When you reflect on the experiences you've had, do you notice any common themes? Can you identify similar or related elements in your work?

  - ¤ **Companies/Organizations:** Where have you worked? What is the typical size or culture that you enjoyed most? Were they private, public, nongovernmental organizations (NGO), or nonprofit?

  - ¤ **Verticals/Industries:** Which sectors do you understand and find intriguing? If you gained most of your experience outside traditional businesses (for instance, working with family as a caregiver or as a homemaker), look for parallels that this work might relate to (for instance, hospitality, client services, or management).

  - ¤ **Functional Areas:** Were you working on activities that could cut across different areas of work (for instance, project management or financial analysis)? These types of skills are often industry-agnostic and may be recognized by different descriptive names. Consider the various ways you have contributed, then research the best way to describe it later.

¤ **Activities:** Which aspects of work do you enjoy doing? Drill down into specific tasks where you excel or derive pleasure, and those you would prefer to avoid.

- **Working Style:** How do you most like to work? What's the right mix of being by yourself or with others (socializing versus private time, alone/independent versus team/collaborative)? Do you prefer more structured versus unstructured, or loud versus quiet environments? These are just a few dimensions, so consider any aspects of when and how you work best.

- **Productive Time:** When do you like to work, and when do you accomplish the most? Are you a morning or an evening person, or do you get the most done midafternoon? Does your current work align with your preferred timing?

Dan, a tech professional with a heavily client-focused job that required a lot of virtual meetings, was stressed-out by his work schedule. While not a morning person, his job required early-morning virtual conference calls without breaks to reset or reflect. During a trip working from a different time zone, he realized how much starting his workday later enabled him to function better and have free morning time. After returning from that trip, he negotiated with his manager to begin his work schedule three hours later, three days a week, to create more space in his day which significantly improved his overall work and life balance.

- **Energy:** What gives you energy? Do you consider yourself an introvert (prefer and need a lot of alone time to concentrate and recharge) or an extrovert (enjoy being around a lot of people, needing active engagement with others to feel inspired and motivated)? How much do you prefer to interact with others or be alone throughout the day? Consider how other people impact your energy.

- **Accommodation:** What do you need to work well? Do you need headphones to reduce external noises or distractions in an open-plan office? Are special tools, technologies, or adaptability required to support your ability to work effectively? Are you comfortable requesting what you need, or does this create challenges? Examples include working from home rather than being in the office or needing a permit or Visa to do work in a specific region.

- **Level of Challenge:** How much challenge do you prefer? What experiences would you like to have to support your growth? Do you enjoy repetition and focus? Would you like to develop a level of mastery? Do you need constant variety and learning new things?

- **Weaknesses:** Where and in which areas do you struggle? Do you have the necessary training in these areas, or are they hard for you to do in general? Which activities take you out of your comfort zone and cause you to struggle?

- **Dislikes:** What situations, challenges, experiences, or types of work would you prefer to avoid? You may be capable of doing these things, but do not enjoy them. This is an important distinction to make—what do you do because you can, not because you enjoy it? Recognize the difference.

- **Reactions:** How do you handle pressure? Does stress fuel you or drain you?

- **Finances:** What are your income requirements to cover your annual expenses? Have you created a budget? Which numbers are most important to you (base salary is typically a consistent monthly amount, whereas bonuses or commissions are often variable and tied to outside factors)? Do you know the minimum amount needed for you to live on? Do you have sufficient savings to cover six months of expenses?

Your Current Personal Situation

- **Relationships:** Are you currently surrounded by people you like? Those whom you spend the most time with will reflect your experience. Do you have supportive friends and family around you?

- **Environment:** Do you like where you live and work? Does your personal living situation—your home, space, lighting, and town—feel supportive? What elements might you want to shift? *Revisit the Conscious Clearing exercise (on page 84) to refresh your memory and see if anything has shifted.*

- **Values:** What do you appreciate? Where do you derive your sense of satisfaction—from personal relationships, or other forms of work and recognition?

- **Impact:** What contribution do you want to make? Where do you want your efforts to matter? In which areas are you most interested in making a difference?

- **Connection:** What gives you a sense of belonging? Who do you like to spend time with, and in what ways?

Your Current Work Situation

- **Current Job:** If you are working (full- or part-time, freelance, volunteering, or other activity), do you like your actual role? How do you feel about the work itself? If you're not working, how are you feeling about your situation? How are you spending your time?

- **Recognition:** Do you have an office or a title that reflects your responsibilities? Do you feel valued and appreciated for your contribution? What makes you feel inspired to work harder?

- **Dislikes:** What do you not like about your job and situation? Which daily activities would you avoid doing, if possible? Where do you feel frustrated?

- **Company:** Do you like the organization and what it stands for? Are they doing work that is important? Do you relate to their products or services?

- **Industry:** Do you like or care about the sector and challenges that your organization is working on or solving? Are you working on addressing meaningful issues? Is the industry broad or narrow? Is it related to where you live or location-agnostic? Are you in the right industry vertical (or function)?

- **Management:** How do you get along with your direct manager or boss? What do you think of senior management or the executive team? Does their style align with your values? Do you feel recognized and valued?

- **Team:** Do you like your peers? How do you get along with your colleagues? What organizational dynamics do you notice, and how do they make you feel?

- **Compensation:** Do you feel fairly paid for your contribution? How is the balance of your salary and bonus (hard dollars) with nonfinancial benefits, like health care, training, or other perks (soft dollars)?

- **Space:** Do you like your work environment? How is your office space (open-plan/remote) and location? Are you completely virtual and working from home, do you commute, or do you work hybrid?

- **Culture:** How is the company culture? Does it feel supportive and collaborative, or political and competitive? Are work relationships collegial?

- **Purpose:** Do you believe in the company's mission? Are their values clear? Do you agree with how they uphold the values?

- **Strategy:** Do you like the company's business approach? Do they have an effective strategy you can get behind?

- **Skills:** Do you have a specialized background? What certifications or specialized skills does the job require? What degree do you have? From which school? Does this matter to you or your job?

- **Stress:** How is the stress level at your current work? Does growth feel exciting or overwhelming? Are your job requirements fixed and structured, or more fluid and flexible? Which do you prefer?

Did you discover anything unexpected in your responses? Were there any surprising reactions or observations that could be important? Make note of the most important realizations you had.

You may enjoy your work, but not like who you're working for; or, conversely, you may believe in the company and its mission but are not in a role suited to your skills or preferences. Maybe you dislike everything about your job, company, and boss, but you have great relationships with your colleagues; or, you love your nonprofit, mission-driven work but would like to earn more. These are all very different situations with different challenges to address.

REALIZE (PART 2)

EXERCISE (Part 2): Life Work Assessment

3. REVIEW YOUR BALANCE

In an ideal world, we are focused on what matters most to us. We spend our time aligned with our values. Let's consider where and how you spend your time during a typical week. You're going to look at your career and work, personal life and self, health and wellness, family, friends, and other aspects of your life. However, if these six categories don't work for you, then customize them to your needs.

Fill in both pie charts below to consider how you spend your time over a typical week (or month). For the chart on the left, decide what you care about, and assign each category a proportion between 0 and 100 percent for how you want to spend your time. Then, in the chart on the right, indicate how much time you currently spend on those activities in a typical week to see what you prioritize, since our actions reflect our beliefs. Ensure the total amounts allocated across all six categories within each circle add up to 100 percent.

Notice the differences between *what you want* and *what you do*. Many clients experience an aha moment seeing the numbers, as they realize how much time they spend on work (particularly for high achievers) over more important personal priorities like family, friends, and travel. Or they discover that, while they think health and wellness is a value, they don't prioritize it in their daily activities. This is an opportunity to reassess where you put your energy, and as a result, how you spend your time.

What we believe or feel is not always truth. For the highly analytical and data-driven, should you wish to measure how you spend your time to see how accurate your predictions were, consider tracking your week. You can use the table below to capture at the end of each day how many hours were spent focused on each of the areas identified. You can either look at the information on a daily or full-week basis to see how you are using your time and get a realistic sense of your current experience.

DAY	1	2	3	4	5	6	7	TOTALS
Date								
Family								
Friends								
Career/ Work								
Personal/ Self								
Health/ Wellness								
Other								
TOTAL (Hours)								

What needs to change? Consider how you might realign your priorities to better reflect your values. As you uncover gaps in how you spend your time now, you can make conscious and intentional shifts to create more satisfaction. Consider where and how you can make subtle or more significant changes to create more alignment in your life and your vision.

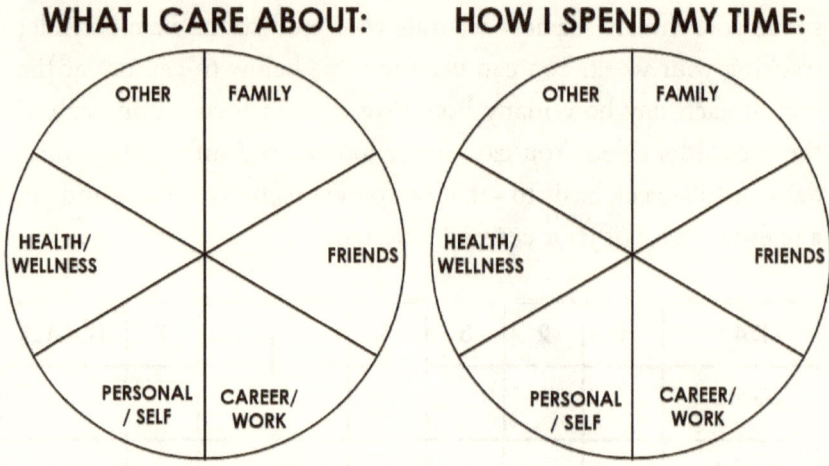

WHAT I CARE ABOUT: ## HOW I SPEND MY TIME:

4. ANALYSIS OF WORK FIT

Now, consider your personal preferences and your current work situation to identify other mismatches in how you spend your time. Are important activities not being incorporated in your work role or perhaps not being appreciated by your organization or manager? You can assess how and what needs to change.

Differentiate between aspects of your current life and work that are *within your control* where you can make different choices, and those that are *outside your control* which may be unchangeable (whether for the moment or in general). For instance, if you must live in a specific location to be near family members, you may not be able to change that. However, if your work hours conflict with other personal interests or obligations, you could explore changing these with your organization to gain more flexibility.

I've seen clients make subtle shifts; for example, doing creative work at night to help them sync with their natural energy and find more flow. Others have required more significant changes, either leaving jobs that were a poor fit or reducing their work week from five eight-hour days to three ten-hour days to free them up for other personal priorities, a side hustle, or traveling to visit family overseas.

The relevant questions here are:

- **Fit:** What's working? What's not working?

- **Control:** What can I change? What can I not change?

Once you determine changes are needed, then you can figure out how either you or your situation needs to shift to support you. Change can't and won't happen if you are unwilling to adjust or explore new ways of being. I've watched burned-out clients continue to overwork rather than make different choices; they felt trapped but were unwilling to consider other options.

Unless we are open to new options, we will keep getting more of the same. It's far better to recognize when something isn't working for whatever reason, than to be forced to change against your will by circumstances.

CLIENT STORY: Career Catapult

When Sarah first came to me for coaching, she was completely burned-out and ready to leave her market research job at a very stressful agency. She had worked there for four years and was ready to make a career switch but wasn't sure where to start.

Together, we worked through multiple aspects of her mindset and reactions, discovering ways that she was inadvertently contributing to her own stress. She had been responding to emails at all hours of the night and on weekends, volunteering to do more work, and not setting any boundaries around her availability—all of which wore her out and made her feel overextended.

In exploring further, we uncovered that Sarah enjoyed collaborating with her colleagues and felt validated when her work was valued by her team. Without consciously realizing it, she was seeking "approval" and acceptance from work, rather than within herself. As her awareness grew, she changed her responses to organize her time better, communicate her needs and boundaries, and stand up for herself.

While she was making these mindset and behavioral shifts to help her manage her current work more effectively, she also started to explore new professional opportunities. Initially, she considered moving from an agency to one of her clients who often had similar positions in-house. She began doing research, reaching out to former colleagues and other professionals to learn about the various options.

In gathering more information, Sarah realized she might not be ready to leave her organization and start all over again. Recognizing she needed to develop additional skills to step into a senior manager role, she decided to advocate for herself within her existing organization.

Six months after we began working together, Sarah was put on the management track and promoted to associate director, increasing her salary to six figures shortly thereafter.

Three years later, Sarah reached out to me again when she was finally ready to leave her company for an external senior position. The ongoing stress and pace of the agency were no longer aligned with how she wanted to live. She felt undercompensated and overworked, and she was ready to start a family. Her networking efforts had paid off, and she was approached by a former colleague for a manager role that would entail a significant increase in responsibility with the commensurate increase in title and salary.

Initially, Sarah was thrilled by this exciting turn of events; however, switching companies would require a relocation, moving closer to the business to work in the office three days per week. This would impact her husband's job, since he would need permission to work remotely from his employer. Together, we explored the pros and cons. A 40 percent salary increase was appealing, but the company's competitive culture and inflexibility on the remote work were red flags. Their human resources department demanded an immediate response, and Sarah made the difficult decision to turn down the job offer since the choice had become very stressful and no longer felt like the right fit.

Sarah continued her search, and within three months, she received a new job offer from another company for a role as a senior manager of market insights at a much larger, more established company which she was excited to work for. All the feedback she received was positive and encouraging without the need to move, and with great health insurance, family leave, and other benefits, not to mention a 63 percent increase in her total compensation.

It was worth the wait! All of Sarah's efforts enabled her to find a more meaningful role that was aligned with her goals. She had built significant leadership skills, managed through challenges, and patiently pursued the best option for her own professional growth and her family—wins all around.

" I knew it was time to make the career jump when I felt the company culture did not align with my personal values. I had given all I had to offer them and taken everything that I could learn from them. Now, I avoid making decisions based on fear. I make a list of pros and cons, and I accept that every career choice will come with ups, downs, and a level of uncertainty—some uncertainties I can anticipate, others will be completely unknown. Accepting the unknown risks helps me to not be afraid of them. Fear exists, and I can manage it! "

—Sarah

Uncover What's Really Going On

We don't always have to know the exact way forward to change our situations. Believing we need certainty is a trick our minds play, trying to maintain old ways of doing things to avoid change, even while other options exist. As we recognize how our actions impact our desired outcomes, new possibilities become available. It's possible to be both strategic and practical to find new opportunities. Idealism and pragmatism can coexist, letting us prioritize our values and avoid rationalizations that want to keep things the same.

Remember, your work now is to experiment and learn by doing. Take risks, see what unfolds, assess, and then adjust accordingly. This process is all about trial and error, facing challenges, and gaining new insights.

See What Is True

Let's explore different issues that may be holding you back—specific or recurring past experiences that may stand in your way, like a wall that you need to break through, climb over, go around, or fly above.

The source of challenges often comes down to two factors: *you* and/or *your situation*. Your goal will be to figure out:

- How *you* contribute to your circumstances, and what elements are within your control (such as your attitude, mindset, reactions, and choices) so you can change them.

- Which *environmental* elements impact you negatively, and whether you can change these. While you can't control the state of the world (the economy, your physical environment, or company culture), you may have the ability or flexibility to leave your company and job. If you must stay for financial or other reasons, then look for other levers to adjust. Use the guidelines below to figure out where you have control.

When Is It You?

- Are you in the *right role*? Does it fit your skills and preferences? Do you have the relevant expertise needed to perform effectively?

- Does it suit your *work style*? Are you in the right structure, and does how your company operates fit your way of working? For instance, introverts often need quiet and don't function well in open-plan office spaces, so they may need to wear headphones or prefer to work remotely to control their workflow and environment.

- Do you like your *job activities*? Are you doing things you enjoy, or things you are good at but don't like to do?

- Do you need to be *challenged* more or are you in over your head? The right amount of stretch feels like inspiring growth. Sometimes, calm and manageable work is preferable to constantly learning new things. However, feeling consistently overwhelmed could be a sign that you may have reached too far, or you've taken on responsibilities that you lack experience in. Could you switch roles or get additional training? Is this possible at your current company, or do you need to go outside?

- Does the job or work match your *expectations*? Some opportunities that seem fabulous on paper can be the wrong fit. Were you lured by things that seemed important (like an office, title, or compensation), only to discover you hate the job, company, or boss? Make sure you know what is most important to you and consider those things that truly matter (like the culture, values, boss, and work itself).

- Do you *believe* in yourself? Self-confidence based on clarity is a superpower that cuts through confusion and ambiguity. Do you know your capabilities and need to trust yourself more? Working for a toxic boss or organization can sap self-confidence when one's value isn't appreciated. Recognize whether you are diminishing yourself, or whether others are blaming you for things outside your scope of responsibility.

Clarify your priorities again to find your *authentic fit filter*: what exactly you need to match future opportunities against. When you know what matters to you, you can follow and trust your inner wisdom, minimize the need to compare yourself to others, and know when you're in the wrong place and move quickly.

When Is It Them?

- Do you have a *bad boss*? Does your work style or background not align with your current manager, or are there other dynamics preventing you from excelling where you are? If you like the company, perhaps you can do an internal transfer to work for someone else. If you need to stay for any reason, you may need to learn how to work with this individual or leave the company to find a better situation.

- Is the *company culture* unsupportive? It can be disheartening to realize you're at a place that doesn't align with your values, perhaps because of nasty internal office politics or other misaligned priorities that won't change. Here, you either need to adapt to stay, or use this knowledge to clarify what you do need. Decide what you won't tolerate or accept in another company. It's difficult to change an organization from within unless you run it, so if your current place of employment isn't supportive, then you might prefer working elsewhere where your skills and expertise are valued.

- Are the *economic, societal, geographic, political, technological, or physical environments* challenging? Are there broader factors at play in the wider market and world impacting your work situation that are completely outside your control? Natural disasters are one example. COVID is another global phenomenon that disrupted many aspects of distribution and supply chains, interpersonal dynamics, travel, health care, and life as we knew it, causing many individuals and organizations to rethink their business models to adapt.

Recognizing and acknowledging what needs to change lets us move toward action. Be willing to face your reality as it is, not as you wish it to be, so you can make thoughtful decisions. Do you sense a recurring theme? *Recognize where you are and what you want to move toward.* Your desires may be unique, and the more you honor them, the clearer your choices will be.

PRACTICE: Recognize Your Situation, Motivation, and Inspiration

You are most likely to engage in and enjoy activities that inspire you. By understanding the underlying drivers of what gives you meaning, you can find work that aligns with your passions.

Listen to and trust your inner guidance and intuition. Consider the following.

- *What inspires you to achieve anything?* Compliments, recognition, respect, responsibility? Which of the following incentives are motivating for you?
  - ¤ Meaningful work (aligned with your values, making a positive contribution)
  - ¤ Compensation (salary, bonus, commission, and equity)
  - ¤ Flexibility and freedom (ability to set your own schedule or work from home)
  - ¤ Health-care benefits (fertility planning, paid time off)
  - ¤ Travel (either as part of your job or sufficient vacation time)
  - ¤ Growth (opportunities to learn and challenge yourself)

- *How would you choose to spend your time?* If you could do anything in the world, without having to worry about money, what would you do?

- *Do you have a personal mission?* How would you like to be of service to bring your gifts forward? If so, what is it? If not, what

might inspire you to make an impact on the world and others? This is closely related to the above question. Consider how you would choose to spend your time if you didn't have to worry about money. This can help uncover those things that give your life meaning and purpose.

- *What would bring you a sense of fulfillment?* Is there an emotional expression that best captures your desires (for instance, happiness, joy, creativity, flow, excitement, challenge)?

CHECK-IN: Be Practical, Safe, and Smart

Since change is often disruptive, minimizing additional uncertainty and creating a sense of security and resiliency can support you in moving through any transition. One way to prepare is by knowing you have sufficient resources available—physically, financially, mentally, and emotionally. In reviewing your life and work situation, do a quick gut check to assess your preparedness and comfort level in managing through change. Be honest with yourself about what safety looks and feels like for you to anticipate and be proactive in managing your process.

Questions to consider are:

- What *risks* are you willing to take? Can you move or change your situation now, or do you need to make things work where you are? Are you ready to share your feelings with friends, family, or partners, or will they not be supportive? If something unexpected happens, like a job loss or an extended period of unemployment, how might you adapt?

- How much *money* do you need to earn or live on? Know your numbers. What are your expenses? Do you have enough of a cushion to support yourself now? Where might you need to cut back or reduce your spending to save more? Differentiate your essential needs from the nice-to-haves. How much do you define your worth by how much you earn, or are other variables also important?

- **What *timeframes* are manageable?** How comfortable would you be with a transition period and uncertainty for longer than three months? Six to nine months? A year or more? Consider your comfort with unpredictable income over time. If you need to be gainfully employed and actively engaged doing something sooner, factor this into your decision-making process to explore alternative or interim financial sources, whether that's a part-time job, personal loan, or accessing savings.

EXERCISE: See It to Be It

You've done a lot of reflection on what you would like; now, it's time to bring it more to life by immersing yourself in the energy of what could be possible if you pursued your dreams and purpose. By clearing your slate of old stuff, you are now prepared for a fresh start. Let's imagine what your life could be like.

> **If my mind can conceive it and my heart can believe it, then I can achieve it.**
> —Muhammad Ali

Visualization is a powerful tool for more clarity, focus, and commitment to your vision. Professional athletes often envision themselves successfully winning races and competitions—helping them prepare mentally, emotionally, physically, and energetically for the experiences they will face to gain an edge. Imagining a successful outcome can impact your attitude and mindset by having you anticipate different outcomes with more clarity before they happen. It's an effective way to train yourself to shift into positivity, like strengthening your muscles through repetitions. Let's begin to explore what would bring you more joy.

Start to see yourself living your juicy master life and work plan, with everything you've ever dreamed of. Let your imagination go wild and trust your heart and intuition around what you desire. *What would your life be and feel like if you could do and have whatever you want?* What sets your heart on fire? Think about the seeds that you want to plant to grow your garden. Visualize, journal, and allow yourself to reflect in your mind's eye on who and how you would like things to be …

- If money were no object, what would you be doing?

- What sort of work and life do you think would light you up?

- How would you want to live?

- What kind of person do you want to be?

- Who are you surrounded by?

- What does your daily life look like?

- How do you spend your time?

While you may have considered these questions before, it's time to elaborate and paint a picture of the life you want to live, making it as full as possible and more tangible. Allow yourself to be immersed in the experience of what you want, to make it so real you can almost taste it.

Bring this image to mind whenever you need a reminder of why you are creating changes in your life right now. We will continue to deepen your vision in future exercises, since it is such an important element of the life you are creating. What you want may shift as you discover more, so allow space for new possibilities to emerge that may be better than you could have even imagined.

RITUAL: Gratitude Practice

What are you grateful for? Positive psychology research studies have shown multiple benefits from establishing an ongoing gratitude practice, from easing depression and improving relationships to enhancing physical and emotional well-being and creating more happiness. Most importantly, gratitude helps to keep things in perspective and create more overall fulfillment.

Today, and perhaps going forward throughout your journey, reflect on three things you are grateful for. Write them down in your journal or notepad to notice what emerges. While initially it may be challenging to find positive things if you are feeling challenged, focus on what you appreciate, even the little things like a sunny day or your favorite tea or cup of coffee in the morning. Recognizing all your senses can bring things to life. What do you see, sense, smell, taste, and feel? Acknowledging what is going well will help you see your progress and notice what has been shifting for you. Observe what happens as you look for more positive aspects of your life and work.

You are making
positive changes!

Appreciate all you
are doing to
create the future
you desire.

RELEASE

CLEAR and ALLOW
Let go of any aspects of your life and work that have been holding you back as you deepen your INNER WORK

CHAKRA: Find your center by connecting with your ROOT chakra

COLOR: RED can bring you more energy and vitality.

ELEMENTS: Ground yourself through connection to the EARTH to feel nourished and whole. Let FIRE burn through anything that you are ready to let go of, purify or compost.

POWER ANIMAL:
SERPENT connects you with your inner power and helps you shed your past to emerge anew.

CRYSTALS:

GARNET can strengthen your connection to your root and support travel.

BLACK TOURMALINE is a highly protective stone that can safeguard your energy field and help ground you more deeply.

TAROT CARDS:

THE DEATH tarot card represents new beginnings and letting go of the past . What things do you need to leave behind so you can be reborn and embrace rebirth?

THE TOWER card is a powerful indicator that it is time to shed old unstable structures and take a leap of faith. Get ready to make way for something new to be rebuilt in its place.

AFFIRMATION:
"I release any unhelpful thoughts, behaviors, patterns or experiences that no longer serve me."

STEP 2: RELEASE

CLEAR AND ALLOW (PART 1)

RELEASE is one of the most powerful steps of the Authentic Alchemy Path because, when completed successfully, clearing creates transformational healing, letting you step forward in a new way with a fresh perspective. This step connects us with the root chakra and our connection to safety.

Your goal is to better understand and address any gaps (or issues from the past) that have been getting in the way of your moving toward. These blocks and challenges can show up as disconnects in aspects of your life that may be preventing you from achieving what you want (your future vision). Resolving them is the support you need to move beyond where you are now (your current situation).

The issues covered in this step are quite comprehensive and may involve considerable reflection, as many are likely to resonate with you. While it would be wonderful to work through everything, it is more than likely you will have one or two key challenges that are most prominently standing in the way of your moving toward what you want. Start by identifying your primary challenge, and focus on that; then, feel free to come back to resolve others.

Each challenge will be followed by a resolution that you can take to help you resolve and address these issues to move forward. As you will see from the example below, individuals can often face multiple challenges in contemplating a change in professional direction.

CLIENT STORY: Entrepreneurial Endeavor

My client, Jeremy, was a happily married father in his forties. After over a decade, his long-term real estate career unexpectedly wound down post-COVID. While he was caught off guard by the change, he also knew it was time for him to move into something different and make a transition. He was ready to explore new options but felt overwhelmed by his choices.

One thing he discovered in spending more time at home with his family was how much he appreciated the flexibility to be with his kids and use his creativity. This was a blessing and a curse as he considered multiple options; he had identified six or more different opportunities that were appealing to him. He was considering building things, teaching, exploring new real estate opportunities, or starting his own business—each with its merits and pitfalls. He also felt pressure to get a traditional corporate job and have a steady paycheck as a practical alternative.

Jeremy had become somewhat paralyzed by his choices, so together, we explored what he really wanted from his work. What had he enjoyed? What was important to him? Where did he struggle? What were his real strengths and interests? Through various practices, I helped him focus and prioritize, looking at why he was drawn to each option. In having him connect viscerally with his body, he was able to explore what felt right or intuitively did not seem like a good fit, and he was able to narrow down his choices to two options.

One option focused on real estate development and house flipping, but he was worried he didn't have the relevant experience. I gave him some growth work to renovate a home bathroom on his own to gain hands-on experience of what the work might be like on a full-time basis through a practical project. He wanted to update this room, anyway, and the project was small enough for him to manage independently. If he didn't like the work, he could shift gears with both a new bathroom and more insight. No foul, no loss.

Our work then uncovered another issue that had been preventing him from choosing a path and moving forward. Jeremy had been holding on to regret over a previous decision. He believed if he had made several different choices in the past, he would be rich and successful now. He had been frustrated and mad at himself for the "one that got away"—something that had been haunting him. Once we reviewed the context, rationale, and benefits he'd gained from his choices at the time, he appreciated his situation and was finally able to release the disappointment he'd been carrying.

Jeremy was able to unwind a knotted rope that had been holding him hostage to an unhelpful narrative that he made poor decisions. Forgiving himself for the past, and acknowledging everything he had achieved, freed him up to trust himself again and take new risks. Several months after this process, I received an exciting update. Jeremy had purchased a small business in memorial retail and property leasing that he was familiar with (yet unrelated to the career choices we had discussed). He understood the business, and it was an opportunity for him to do his own thing with both the freedom and the risks. He was thrilled and excited to embark on this next step of his journey.

Your RELEASE process will be unique to your challenges and issues. In Part 1 of this step, I will be guiding you through the seven chakras to explore various aspects of your life and experience to start creating positive change. Part 2 of this step includes additional rituals and practical strategies to support you in going deeper around the RELEASE process on your own.

As you move through each section, you will begin uncovering and addressing various challenges you may be experiencing, so notice what arises, and prepare to let go of what may be impacting or hindering your growth. After the description of each section, work through the suggested resolution to discover new strategies that can support you in shifting your patterns, changing your mindset, and clearing your energy.

This is arguably among the most important steps on your growth path—overcoming what has been holding you back from moving forward toward more meaning and purpose—which is why this section is so comprehensive. While there are suggestions for how to move through challenges, please recognize that this is deep work I often do with private clients with great sensitivity and care over time. Facing and addressing old wounds is not to be undertaken lightly and should be given the attention, intention, and gentleness that it demands.

While it's possible to heal ourselves, deep trauma and other entrenched patterns and behaviors may be difficult to recognize, acknowledge, and release. If you feel uncertain, get stuck, or feel overwhelmed by this process, please seek professional support. A trauma-informed coach, therapist, or experienced healer can hold a safe space for you to work through any challenges that arise.

Many rituals have been included for you to do independently; however, you also may be too close to your own experience to have perspective or be able to create healthy distance to let go. Be kind to yourself and go slowly as you uncover anything that may be more than you feel equipped to handle on your own.

Coaching or therapy can provide compassionate witnessing

to facilitate and support your discovery process, bringing an unbiased point of view that can honor your journey toward more empowerment and agency. While I love supporting clients, I also believe in your power to heal yourself, which is why the exercises are shared here for you to explore on your own.

The goal is to release unhealthy attitudes, bad experiences or memories, and unhelpful patterns so these don't get trapped and stored in your body as either stress and/or physical pain that can ultimately lead to health issues and illness. Unaddressed repeated stressors can embed in your energy field and cause you to get off-kilter, like a record needle that gets stuck in a groove, damaging the music's fidelity.

Uncovering and dealing with stress and personal challenges now may help you avoid longer-term implications. Don't let untreated issues evolve into physical symptoms (back pain, headaches, burnout, cancer) or professional losses (such as getting laid off, getting fired, or being replaced by technology in your job). Proactively addressing things that feel "off" now can redirect your path toward more positive outcomes.

Going through the RELEASE Process

You will be guided to work your way down the body from your head, starting with the crown chakra, to your base, the root chakra. Each section from one to seven has a series of elements for you to consider and is then followed by the resolution step. You may wish to journal for each section and notice what thoughts, emotions, reactions, bodily sensations, or other intuitive knowing arise as you read through. It is possible that you may feel strongly about each section, or that a few will feel more directly related to your experience than others.

Let's explore which elements are influencing you. Remember to go slowly and be gentle with yourself.

1. MINDSET: Unhelpful Beliefs (Crown Chakra)

What thoughts do you hold that limit your possibilities? The crown chakra connects you with your mind and a higher power. Below are some examples of the types of thoughts that you might have that are unhelpful to you and inadvertently hold you back.

- Do you *worry* what others think (family, friends, religion, local community)? This is a preoccupation with external perceptions and appearances.

- Do you *mistrust* others, yourself, or your situation? This may show up as not believing you can have what you want or that you can rely on anyone else.

- Are you constantly looking to be *valued*? This may appear as seeking a sense of belonging through your connections and relationships (for instance, feeling a need to do whatever is needed or required to fit in, get along and be appreciated by your chosen circle). This may include family, where you have inadvertently taken on roles to help others (parents or siblings) to create more ease, perhaps diminishing your own capabilities, not wanting to outshine them or not believing siblings or parents can be happy for you (which may or may not be true).

- Are you preoccupied by the need to *contribute*? You may find motivation to do things by defining your value in relation to doing things for others. For instance, do you intentionally make decisions and choose actions so your efforts will be acknowledged, and you can feel seen and appreciated?

- Are you motivated by providing *benefit* to others? Do you choose your actions believing you must be of service or support to others. Notice whether you might be perpetuating any unhealthy, codependent, or dysfunctional patterns without realizing it. Do you feel burned out because you are doing things for others that you don't want but rationalize the need to stay and continue through a sense of obligation? Sometimes, we inadvertently play roles for others to give ourselves meaning and purpose. Where or how have you chosen unhealthy relationships because they make you feel appreciated on some level?

- Are your actions or decisions driven by *insecurity*? Are you afraid that you lack the experience and credibility needed to succeed, or do you believe you are not good enough (more about this appears in Part 2 as well)? Do you believe that you must know the answers to control your situation to feel safe?

RESOLUTION: Ditch the Doubts and Choose Your Thoughts
You have the ability in every moment to choose what to think. Negative, uncontrollable thinking—particularly when you constantly doubt yourself—is unhelpful, not to mention demeaning. Positivity combined with pragmatism (think practical optimism) is the name of the game.

Your goal is to become aware of your critical thoughts, call them out in that moment, and then consciously choose to change them to something more empowering. One way to reframe negative self-talk is by reinforcing your commitment to your path, knowing that whatever arises is an opportunity for you to learn.

I've had multiple clients who were former athletes and were used to constantly competing. A need to win often pushed them to be very self-critical, seeing the worst in any situation or criticizing themselves when they weren't at the top of their game. Keith, a successful and ambitious salesperson in his twenties, felt overwhelmed by organizational changes at the tech company he worked for. His persistent drive to achieve hit the limitations of post-COVID market conditions as the business continued to struggle. He had managed to stay employed through several layoffs yet kept pushing to get ahead and move forward.

Once Keith recognized how his internal pattern of critical self-talk was creating anxiety and was not accurately reflecting his external reality, he could step back. He could see how he was running on a hamster wheel nonstop but could choose to step off and stop spinning to center himself more. It was his choice. In getting out of his head and connecting more with his body, Keith became more grounded and was able to respond more easily to his work situation. He discovered he had more control around his choices than he'd realized.

Rather than internalize your negativity, consider giving your doubting voice a name (for example, Critical Chris or Judging Jackie) to externalize it. Acknowledging when your doubting critic shows up, and giving it love for protecting you, can neutralize unconscious reactions and make your choices more intentional. Once you've recognized what (or who) is causing you to react, you can then choose to move forward anyway, without believing that voice's judgment.

You might want to have conversations with different aspects of yourself to better understand their reactions, and to explain why you are choosing to act differently now. These are some examples of how to work with your inner child, parts and Internal Family Systems, and approaches pioneered by Richard Schwartz, among others. This is deep and powerful work beyond the scope of this book, and it can be an effective way to understand different aspects of yourself.

Since the crown chakra also relates to your connection to spirit or the divine, consider your relationship to source and a higher power. How might you learn to trust the universe more fully? What would it take for you to feel safe and believe in what's possible? How does your mind's need to control keep you from knowing you can manage and respond to whatever arises?

2. VISION: Not Trusting Your Inner Wisdom (Third Eye)

When do you ignore your inner vision? This section connects with your third-eye chakra, which symbolizes your connection to your insight and what you see. Do you have a poor attitude toward life, or can you go within and believe in your experience?

Here are some ways that you may experience intuitive challenges:

- Are you a *perfectionist?* Do looks matter? Do you feel the need to keep up appearances or to have complete control over every aspect of your life to feel safe? This can show up as impostor syndrome and never being satisfied, or as believing that what you have, what you've done, or who you are isn't sufficient unless it looks picture-perfect.

- Do you *willfully ignore* your abilities and not have a realistic sense of your limitations? This might show up as feeling entitled to certain privileges, favoritism, and treatment, or as intentionally denying or avoiding dealing with areas where you struggle. What idiosyncrasies are you perpetuating? Often, others will notice things that we tend to overlook because they make us uncomfortable, like the metaphorical "elephant in the room."

- Do you find yourself constantly succumbing to *peer pressure?* Looking outside yourself to see what others are doing can be a subtle trap where you constantly compete with a group of friends who make you feel insecure or unable to be happy. You might judge appearances on the outside and feel frustrated that you are not living up to what others have achieved.

- Do you experience *conflicted* emotions or ambivalent feelings? These can occur when there's a disconnection between what you see, say, and think, which causes you to send mixed messages because you're unaware of or haven't acknowledged how you really feel. Do you take a different perspective from others to avoid addressing differences, or do you overlook red flags because you don't like conflict? How might you not be seeing where your dreams and lived experience are not in sync to avoid discomfort? This is where idealism (or willful blindness) may be getting in the way of practicality.

- Do you *compare yourself to others*? Constantly looking outside yourself, rather than going within to trust your own intuition, can cause unhappiness. Do you feel dissatisfied with what you've achieved (in terms of title, salary, prestige) when considering your progress relative to peers, siblings, parents, other family members, social media influencers, or celebrities, even when these standards may not be realistic? Do you believe you come up short, or feel surrounded or overwhelmed by societal pressure from friends, peers (needing to keep up with the Joneses), your religion, community, or the capitalist work ethic?

Three distinct ways this shows up:

- ¤ **Not Being Enough:** Feeling "less than," or that you haven't achieved what you expected, lived up to others' expectations, or don't have the same ambition or perceived prestige (for instance, needing an Ivy League or advanced degree).
- ¤ **Not Having Enough:** Measuring your success by material possessions and things (wanting to win by dying with the

most toys). Constantly pursuing more and focusing on tangible external markers and validators such as income, title, power, and authority.

¤ **Not Doing Enough:** Getting caught up in the rat race and a constant need to work harder to prove yourself to others. Feeling guilty over not working long enough hours or feeling an ingrained push to constantly be "doing," defining yourself and living by hustle culture.

RESOLUTION: Look in the Mirror and Notice Your Blind Spots
Our third eye controls not just our sight, but our vision and ability to believe what we see and feel intuitively. Our experiences often reflect where we focus our energy and attention. People and things that generate strong reactions in us or activate us can bring to the surface important information for us to become aware of.

Take a few moments to reflect on your positive and negative triggers (specific people, experiences, emotions, reactions) that get you worked up and cause you to feel strongly.

- *Who or what situations bring you down?* When do you become upset, get angry or aggravated, or withdraw and shut down emotionally or energetically? Try to identify as many specifics as possible and notice any recurring patterns. Strong and unexpected reactions often point to hidden or unacknowledged (shadow or disowned) aspects of yourself, both good and bad. You may judge aspects of yourself that you notice in others that are hard for you to see or accept. We often will continue to be triggered until we can accept how this experience shows up in our lives and can acknowledge it and integrate it.

- *Who inspires you?* Individuals whom you admire, look up to, or find intriguing can be role models or represent aspects of yourself that you don't fully own. Can you reclaim these parts of yourself to incorporate them more fully into who you are?

Everyone carries a shadow, and the less it is embodied in the individual's conscious life, the blacker and denser it is. At all counts, it forms an unconscious snag, thwarting our most well-meant intentions.
—Carl Jung

Notice strong internal or intuitive reactions to things and internal disconnects between your thoughts and feelings. Feeling conflicted is an important clue that your beliefs and feelings may be out of sync and that further reflection may be warranted.

If (or when) you deny your feelings, notice why you won't trust your intuition. For instance, have you ignored or overridden any hunches about situations or individuals that felt a little "off," but you rationalized or decided not to follow your gut? Do you willfully overlook aspects of yourself, your situation, or perhaps your family or friends group to fit in, get along, or get ahead?

The key here is to look at reality so you can be practical and make conscious choices, rather than living in fantasy or avoiding seeing things as they really are. Remind yourself of your vision to stay positive in the face of challenges, by committing to the future you want to see. Making progress on your intentions will make it easier to envision your new reality.

3. STORIES: Unhelpful Messages (Throat)

What narrative do you tell yourself? Do you support and build yourself up, or do you tear yourself down? Does a critical inner voice diminish your self-worth? This section connects with the throat chakra, which represents your voice and ability to speak your truth.

Notice what you tell yourself and how it might directly influence your experience.

- Which *old stories* do you continue to tell that are no longer true? Are there past beliefs you keep repeating out of habit, or ingrained patterns that you have outlived and need to let go of? For example, believing in a puritanical/capitalist work ethic that says work has to be hard, or an early experience that made you feel that you don't deserve joy, may hinder your ability to create positive change with ease.

- Do you have ingrained and recurring *ancestral patterns* or generational family restrictions or expectations that may hold you back? This can include cultural tales like the "tall poppy syndrome" that you will get cut down for rising above others, or believing your family is cursed and doesn't have any luck in business. What stories does your family have about money, success, or work that you may have taken on?

- Do you have a mean *inner critic*? The voices in our heads can be very nasty and can come out through judgment of ourselves and others. What unhelpful things do you say to yourself that shut you down or remind you of your fears? If you don't notice them, consider asking a friend or partner whether they've heard you be hard on yourself or others.

- Are you *silent* when you should be saying something? The inability to speak up or out happens when your voice is frozen, whether as stage fright, stammering, or being unable or uncomfortable articulating what you think. Introverts can find it challenging to express themselves in large groups when surrounded by more aggressive or overwhelming personalities, which can undermine their confidence. Be aware of whether you are choosing not to speak, or if some inner voice is shaming you or holding you back from sharing your truth.

- What is your relationship to *noise* and *self-expression*? How comfortable are you standing up for yourself when you're surrounded by other strong personalities? Are you able to get into the fray and share your perspective, or do you prefer to withdraw and hide? Where and when do you notice this dynamic?

- Do you experience *confusion* or uncertainty when you try to express yourself? Are you struggling to find the right words to express who you are, what you do, or what you believe? This may be some part of you that is uncomfortable owning your value.

- Are you *demanding* of yourself and others? Making demands, threatening others with ultimatums or otherwise creating combative interactions can be a defense mechanism and is not helpful in building relationships and connections.

RESOLUTION: Release the "Shoulds"

Your voice holds power and is an important instrument to share your perspective with the world. Notice ways you mute yourself and hold yourself back or inadvertently try to silence others to control them. Was being quiet, seen but not heard, a virtue in your family? Were you shot down for speaking up, so you learned to stay quiet and keep your opinions to yourself? Subtle and subversive, fear and/or shame are powerful underlying emotions that might be stopping you from sharing your truth.

- **Shoulding Yourself:** Recognize old stories you tell yourself (and there may be several) about how things "should" be that are no longer true. Interrogate your thoughts to notice whether you are repeating what someone else told you and question those assumptions. That may be their experience, but it doesn't need to be yours. Ask yourself why you believe this, and whether it's true. Replace "should" with a positive perspective that feels more accurate and truthful. Notice and separate from the belief of what you should do and feel into your body to see what wants to be expressed.

- **Shoulding Others:** Also notice when you might tell yourself (or someone else) what they should do. Write it down, then ask yourself why you're doing it. Who thinks you or they should do this thing, and is it true? Where did that message come from? Do they have to? Who told you, and what is perpetuating that inner voice? Is the criticism affirming or shaming? Rephrase critical communications to be less judgmental, such as, "Would you consider …?" Questions are invitations that open space for possibility, not commands that demand acquiescence.

As you uncover hidden stories that may be sabotaging you, see them for what they are (old experiences that have outlived their usefulness). You can develop more helpful responses that support what you want to create. Learn to trust yourself by taking smaller risks to speak up. Notice when, where, and around whom you feel safe. Decide how much you care what someone else thinks, or whether your perspective is more important and worthy enough to be shared regardless of their opinion.

Many of us are taught from a young age that our feelings don't matter. Some learn to only speak when spoken to and are discouraged from standing out. Others are expected to excel at everything and receive criticism for being less than perfect in any area (I've seen this with many immigrants, for example, from Eastern Europe and Asia, who have moved countries and want to fit in and are particularly focused on work and professional achievements).

Parents often want to protect their children and may reinforce historical family patterns that become assimilated without question. Unless we become aware and believe other possibilities are true, it can be difficult to question unstated assumptions. Ingrained beliefs are sneaky and subtle in how they can permeate our thinking without question. Bravery is needed to tell new stories that challenge fixed worldviews. There is a risk that others may become uncomfortable being questioned, yet this is how change starts.

Fairy tales are old myths that were designed to teach lessons, invoke fear, and protect us from danger. For example: don't go into the woods, or the big bad wolf will eat you (Little Red Riding Hood); watch out for dangerous gifts from evil queens (Snow White); and don't trust unfriendly stepmothers and stepsisters (Cinderella). We may not recognize when we have internalized and perpetuated false stories that were created to serve a purpose but no longer speak to our reality.

Once we notice how we may be limiting ourselves by not sharing our perspectives, we can create new narratives around participation and contribution. You can choose new actions. Stretch beyond your current assumptions.

Consider asking for what you want in low-risk situations, like at a restaurant, then build up to requesting more in higher-stakes situations, like countering unrealistic work deadlines or requesting a salary increase. Positive experiences and small successes build over time and can help you overcome your doubts. Engaging in meaningful activities that build your experience will give you confidence to talk about your perspective.

Working with affirmations is another way to replace critical messages such as, "I don't have anything interesting to say," or, "No one wants my opinion," with more empowering statements such as, "My perspective is valuable," and, "Other people appreciate when I share my thoughts." Once you notice and become aware of what's not working, then you can create new, more empowering messages that support what you wish to believe and how you want to become in the future. You can start rewiring your internal messaging and brain in new ways.

Stories you created in the past were meant to keep you, your ego, and your feelings safe. Until you can acknowledge, question, and overcome these old narratives, they will drive your life, like a hidden operating system with a bug that is running the show and is keeping you stuck. Once you see which messages may be blocking you, you can start to change them. Know this work may not happen overnight, and it requires practicing love and compassion for yourself.

4. ATTACHMENTS: Holding On (Heart)

Do you have healthy, supportive relationships? Often, we form deep connections to people, places, and things because they are symbolic and represent safety and security in our minds. Some attachments are valuable and life-affirming, while others may become habituated, outlive their purpose, and keep us stuck or trapped in unhelpful ways.

Attachments often occur in the heart chakra, our central source of relating to others and the world. Are we open or closed to possibilities? Can we trust others and ourselves? Consider the various relationships, connections, and ways you engage with and hold on to others to make yourself feel safe. Notice whether your current approach is serving you or holding you back from moving forward in ways that can be more supportive.

- Do you feel *disconnected?* Are there ways you separate or distance yourself from others or even yourself? Feeling insecure or that you don't belong can make you feel different or unusual or make it challenging to fit in. Recognize what you are longing for and why you may be holding back.

- Do you lack healthy *boundaries?* Do you feel safe and respected physically? Individuals with open or porous energy fields lack buffers or barriers to protect themselves from unwanted intrusions. This can happen for those with family members who needed continual reassurance. Do you derive value through connection and unintentionally give your energy and attention to others without setting limits? Collectivist cultures encourage community connection and can de-emphasize individuation, prioritizing the needs of the family or wider group. Being constantly permeable can be draining, result in self-negation, or lead to burnout as one's energy becomes depleted.

- Are you a *people pleaser*? Do you need to be liked at all costs? Do you avoid conflicts or feel uncomfortable with any form of criticism (either giving or receiving it)? Collegial relationships are important, but being unwilling or unable to address differences can bypass important issues that may require resolution.

- Does *fear* drive your choices? Fear can show up in many forms, from fear of failure or rejection to fear of success, responsibility, visibility, surpassing family, or change. All these concerns may arise at different times for many of us.

- Do you have an unhealthy sense of *responsibility* for others? This can show up as the obligation to put others' needs above your own or take on others' emotional burdens by not letting them take care of themselves. Many family dynamics can result in parents taking care of children or siblings at their own expense, or vice versa.

- How do you *hide* by diminishing your own success? Do you hold back, withdraw, keep yourself small, or avoid standing out from the crowd? Families with strong or dominant matriarchs or patriarchs can discourage differences and demand conformity and compliance. It can feel safer to "not make waves," than to show up fully.

- Do you feel *unsafe* trusting others? If you experienced a previous betrayal, or if someone took advantage of your good nature, you may have resistance to engaging with others or believing they are acting with good faith.

- How attached are you to an *old identity*? Have you been defining yourself by a previous role that gave your life purpose or meaning that you can't let go of? We can become attached to personal brands or things we were once known for. Career switchers can find it particularly hard to let go of how they were recognized previously when they feel less confident about a new or unknown path. Cultivating a new way of being takes time, but holding on to a past you no longer desire can be restrictive and can prevent you from moving toward what you want.

RESOLUTION: Replace Criticism with Self-Acceptance

The heart wants what the heart wants, but if it's shut down, then it becomes hard to feel. When you notice that you are feeling something deeply that's uncomfortable, return to the present moment. Where you are right now is the sum of all your past experiences and those you have yet to embrace. You are an amazing amalgamation of every aspect of your being. Who you are and what you have to offer matters and has significance. Know that your value and identity are not defined by what you did before, or by things you don't yet understand or haven't mastered.

Notice when you are being harsh with yourself or others. How can you bring more love and understanding to all your key relationships, and foremost, to yourself? Recognize what you do well and make conscious choices to bring more awareness to patterns that keep you from your full expression.

For those seeking new opportunities, it can be common to focus on past experiences without relating to the current requirements. This indicates an attachment to the past without recognizing the possibilities in the future. The more you are connected to who you were, the less you have embraced who you want to be. While it's natural to talk about a favorite job or company, an old skill set, or a specialized degree you obtained, notice if everything you are communicating is focused on the past. Make a conscious decision to look toward the future and imagine new opportunities.

It's important to recognize when you are idealizing something that no longer exists because it takes you away from where you are now (the present moment) and what you hope to create in the future. Think of this analogy: would you enjoy being on a date with someone who kept talking about their ex? While they may have showed up with the intention of meeting someone new, their words and messaging indicate their attachment to the past. It's unlikely they will be ready to entertain something new.

How important is it to continue defining yourself by how you were before? Are you ready to explore new ways of being? You can honor your background, previous experiences, and people and things that have contributed to who you are now (your family, culture, etc.) while still releasing old ways of being that are no longer helpful. It may be time to just *do you, boo*. Supporting yourself can start with a fan club of one—*you!*

5. BEHAVIORS: Unhelpful Actions (Solar Plexus)

How well do you manage yourself and your reactions? How we act and react are responses to our thoughts and emotions. Sometimes, we can find ourselves at the mercy of stressful circumstances that cause us to respond in unhelpful ways. We must come from a place of awareness to break away from destructive reactions, like getting defensive or aggressive, pushing others away, or withdrawing.

Our inner power resides within our solar plexus chakra. Just as getting physically punched in the gut can knock us down, unexpected experiences can catch us off guard and cause a similar emotional or energetic reaction. I invite you to explore, without judgment, how your responses may be hijacked and cause unhelpful or explosive interactions, rather than positive and affirming ones, in the following areas.

- Do your *emotions* control you? Are you often at the mercy of strong feelings and reactions, or are your actions thoughtful and considered? Have you experienced a strong knee-jerk defensive reaction or gotten easily offended at something? Consider what circumstances set you off to notice your underlying patterns. Four reactions typically occur in the face of challenges: fighting (becoming aggressive), fleeing (running away), fawning (making "nice" to avoid conflict), or freezing (becoming still or stuck). These protective responses can help you avoid feeling pain but can also become unproductive, depending on the situation.

- How does *anxiety* impact you? Overwhelming negative thoughts or excessive stress can overload our capacity to deal. When stress is unaddressed, it leads to burnout, exhaustion, depression, or accidents.
    - ¤ For many years, my signal of being overwhelmed was when I started bumping into walls. It was funny and embarrassing, but when my work became incredibly stressful, I would kick into overdrive, move too quickly, and start banging into people and things. This was my body's way of letting me know I was anxious. It was my cue to slow down and be more mindful to avoid a bigger accident. Thankfully, I no longer run a mile a minute, and I haven't experienced this pattern in a long time; however, if this response reappears, I will know my stress is increasing.

- Are you constantly in *competition* with others? Having a win-at-all-costs mentality can drive one to want to get ahead regardless of the consequences. Athletes often develop competitive mindsets that, while helpful in sports and perhaps great in sales roles, can be counterproductive in work situations that require collaboration. Comparing yourself to others with different experiences, goals, or skills can prevent you from focusing on your own progress and performance as you look outside yourself to measure success.

- Are your efforts an attempt to minimize *shame*? Guilt can occur in response to accidents or mistakes, while shame is an internalized sense of blame. When we do something wrong, act inappropriately, or worry about being judged by others, we can become overwhelmed by feelings of humiliation or embarrassment, whether what we experienced was within our control or not. Are old slights or hurtful, embarrassing memories inadvertently holding you back from taking future risks?

- Where do you feel *powerless*? Are there ways you feel you lack agency or self-determination? Disempowerment can arise for various reasons, including structural issues (such as historical perceptions of gender, race, sexual preference, age, or physical ability) that cause people to feel disadvantaged or without power. Recognizing where and how you have control can be helpful in regaining your ability to impact your future.

- Do you have *unhelpful habits* or unproductive ways of operating that keep you stuck? Have you fallen into any routines that prevent you from changing things up, or are you experiencing inertia that keeps you where you are? Other examples could include arriving late to meetings, demeaning others or yourself, backstabbing, overpromising and underdelivering, or overcommitting and not following through. Being stubborn, acting like a martyr, being unwilling to ask for help, or needing to be right all the time are additional behaviors that may have helped you navigate past challenges but can work against you and become counterproductive now.

- Have you suffered from *trauma*? This can occur in multiple ways. Three primary sources include:

  ¤ *Previous experiences* or painful interactions that impacted you energetically. For example: at work you could have had a bad boss; been at the wrong corporate culture; experienced a layoff, economic disruption, or other physical dislocation; been furloughed; placed in the wrong role that didn't match your skills; or recognized your style wasn't appreciated where you were. Perhaps you had an accident or an upsetting childhood interaction. Imprints from these memories or situations can stay with you and hold you back. Notice whether previous experiences might cause you to avoid things now.

  ¤ *Ancestral* trauma occurs when familial or generational patterns that occurred before your birth are repeated. Bruce Lipton has done extensive work in epigenetics, demonstrating how families that survived war or health issues have passed these characteristics on to subsequent generations. This can show up in other repeated family patterns that impact our experiences.

  ¤ *Past-life* experiences (also known as karma) can carry over into this lifetime. These patterns may be difficult to identify or understand, particularly for those who may not believe in this possibility; however, past-life experiences can represent recurring soul-level challenges without other recognizable causes that are meant to be addressed and resolved in this lifetime.

RESOLUTION: Forgiveness Ritual

Making mistakes is part of living. If we didn't fall, then we wouldn't know how to get back up, just as young children learn how to walk. We also must overcome setbacks and find ways to move forward after difficult experiences. This is the practice of learning how to forgive ourselves when something didn't go the way we hoped or intended. And when possible, to forgive others who may have harmed us, recognizing that this does not condone past experiences but releases the energy from that harm which could be keeping us trapped in the past.

Are there any upsetting experiences, mishaps, or mistakes you recall that you are holding on to or that still may be weighing you down, held in the back of your mind, or that emerge under stress? Can you acknowledge what you learned from them? Finding lessons from your experiences, no matter how difficult or challenging, can help you to reframe what happened. Remember to get the support you need to move through painful past incidents if this feels overwhelming to do on your own. Once you recognize what you learned, you can make different choices now about how to act going forward.

It may also be important to *reframe your language*. How do you speak about your past experiences? While you may believe you really f*cked something up, consider stating that differently, perhaps as something that didn't work out as you'd hoped and acknowledging that it enabled you to make different choices now. When possible, minimize and try to avoid reinforcing negative beliefs (for instance, that you are incapable of overcoming challenges). You can now approach any challenges with a new perspective; the past does not need to define you. Your valuable lessons will serve you well in the future.

Review one thing you learned from something that didn't work out the way you'd hoped. Can you forgive yourself or the other person and let it go? One option to formalize this ritual is writing a letter to this person, or yourself, saying whatever you need to get off your chest. Writing is a powerful way to express things we may not feel comfortable saying out loud. Then, afterward, you can (safely) burn what you wrote, and say a prayer or an intention to release the past, and watch it disappear into the smoke. You can also rip up the paper into shreds and bury it or throw it away.

Using the elements in your rituals here can be particularly

useful. Fire is fast-acting, where air can blow things away or earth would support slower grounding of any process. It's not necessary to send or share your letter with anyone. You can still experience the release which comes from simply acknowledging what happened and writing it out without censoring yourself.

Another option, if you prefer talking to writing, is to pretend you are having a conversation with the person (or yourself). You may choose to speak aloud (to yourself, or even to an empty chair or a tree). Should you feel ready to approach the person to clear the air, you could make a phone call (better than an email or a text which don't always get delivered) or schedule a meeting to share what is on your mind. You may want to practice beforehand to get clear about your intentions.

Defining and reminding yourself of your goals for what you hope to achieve can be helpful in remembering your purpose. Do they need to be present to listen without responding, or are you seeking a conversation and dialogue? When you notice yourself wanting to hurt or shame others or yourself, consider that more reflection may be needed. Remember, this ritual is for your healing, so trust however you feel to go through a process that feels supportive for you. Mostly, this is about forgiving yourself to make more space for what you want; it's not about them.

Your solar plexus is your center and the source of your power. Since it can be easily impacted by others' criticisms or attempts to take you down, you can protect yourself by strengthening this area through how you show up. As you build your confidence through self-awareness and experience, you will become more whole and integrated. As you practice showing up for yourself, you will feel more empowered to stand up for yourself, which will benefit you in everything you do.

6. BLOCKS: Lack of Creativity or Passion (Sacral)

What are you passionate about? Your inner motivation to create is one of the most important sources of your drive and is the inspiration for art, innovation, and anything new in the world. Your ability to explore and develop new ideas resides within the sacral chakra. You can locate this area in the womb space (the source of birth both physically and literally for new ideas to be born in women), and in the *hara* or *dantian* (an energetic source of power located directly below the belly button, recognized in Eastern energy medicine modalities) for all humans and men.

Notice whether you feel creatively resourced to develop and pursue your ideas. Do you let yourself connect with your passions and interests?

- Do you have a *fear* of visibility that causes you to hide, preventing you from putting your work or yourself out in public? Perhaps you are afraid of judgment or criticism. It can be scary to be seen in your truth and have others know who you really are, and yet, this is the work you are here to do.

- Do you experience strong *feelings* or emotions that arise without warning? These reactions can control you, and they often signal a deeper underlying issue to look at. Consider whether your responses are legitimate, or if they may be happening due to other physical (hormonal) or psychological reasons that merit further exploration.

- Do you find yourself *faking* things to hide your true self? Have you chosen to say one thing or act a certain way, rather than be honest? While using subterfuge or dissembling may seem helpful in the short term in certain circumstances, it's not a great long-term strategy to be authentic, and it can become an unhelpful habit that disconnects you from yourself.

- Do you encounter *creative blocks* that prevent you from accessing your true expression? Explore what might be contributing to any malaise or lack of inspiration, whether it's a specific incident, an unhelpful thought, or a fear getting in the way that you need to turn around.

- Are you *disconnected* from your intuition? Do you dismiss your own inner wisdom or not listen to your instincts? Have you denied your feelings in the past or not allowed yourself to rely on your own impressions? Look at why it might be uncomfortable to believe in yourself.

- Do you experience *insecurity* from lack of confidence or uncertainty, not trusting yourself or your circumstances? Have previous challenging circumstances caused you to feel helpless or unsure, even when things are going well?

RESOLUTION: Move It Out, Around, and Through

Your sacral chakra is inherently tied to creativity and movement, so any form of active engagement of your whole body will help to loosen and unblock it. Walking, dancing, playing, shaking, skipping, or active sports activities will get your energy flowing. Physical movements help to overcome inertia.

If you feel blocked, go outside for a walk, or put on some great music and dance. Shimmy. Skip. Jump rope. Do some jumping jacks. See what opens as you connect to your body; notice how you feel. Being fully in your body will help you access more self-expression and will free your mind to wander. See how long it takes to change your perspective: five or ten minutes, thirty minutes, or an hour? Take whatever time is needed to get out of your head and land in your body.

If you work long hours at your job, sitting at a desk or not taking breaks, you could become disconnected from your body. Have you stopped exercising or meeting your physical needs (drinking water, taking bathroom breaks, or eating regularly)? Get up from your desk, and go out for a walk or a jog to return to your center. Even taking a coffee or tea break and a full-body stretch can be good, not just for your health, but also for your mindset.

When you notice frustration, aggravation, stress, doubt, or criticism setting in, take a time-out. Stop. Get up. Move or shift where you are sitting and what you are doing. Explore something else. Get back to positivity. Ground. Notice how you interpret your emotions. Are you anxious, overwhelmed, or stressed yet able to cope? Learn to recognize the signs of burnout before they manifest to help you avoid destabilizing yourself.

7. EXPERIENCES: Lack of Safety (Root)

Do you feel safely grounded? Finding stability and security within ourselves and our surroundings is a fundamental need to feel safe, not in constant fight-or-flight mode. It's hard to find our balance when we're floating on a rocky ship. Even after the waves have passed, we can still feel queasy and unsettled physically, emotionally, mentally, and energetically.

Safety and security are deeply connected to our root chakra, which represents our sense of grounding in the world. Can we stabilize ourselves amid uncertainty, or do we become easily unmoored by situations that feel beyond our control?

Explore where you struggle to feel secure in your experiences.

- Do you have a *scarcity* mentality or a history of loss? Experiences of uncertainty can cause us to hold on to what we have and prevent us from taking risks or investing in ourselves. If you lost something of value, you might over index on safety and security because you fear losing things again. Understand your tolerance for risk and notice when any beliefs around lack become immobilizing or prevent you from moving forward.

- Do you have *financial* security? The ability to earn a living, cover expenses, have a roof over your head, and feel stable is a fundamental and practical need. Experiencing a financial loss or setback in the past can be unsettling. Do you have enough money in savings to allow you to explore new opportunities? Can you reduce your expenses to adapt to changing circumstances? Assess how much money is enough to help you feel resourced.

- Do you feel *ungrounded* at times? Have you reacted to challenges by leaving your body energetically? It's possible to be physically present yet withdraw emotionally or energetically. This response can happen if you felt unsafe in the past because of previous experiences of betrayal, abuse, or trauma, and it feels safer to leave your body. Learning how to stay in your body instead of fleeing when fear arises takes courage and practice. Grounding tools and embodiment practices can support you in coming back to yourself.

- Do you feel *stuck*? The need for safety can cause you to freeze, feel overwhelmed, and stay where you are. The fear of change or worry that things will be worse elsewhere can prevent you from moving forward. If you notice you are avoiding things and find it easier to do nothing, recognize any unhelpful underlying thought patterns and assumptions.

RESOLUTION: Grounding Practices

There are various ways to feel more centered in yourself. Meditation and breath work (particularly deep diaphragmatic breathing) can bring stillness to your mind and body. These practices can be helpful for when you are sitting on a mat. You also need to learn how to calm your nervous system in daily life when you are facing unexpected stressors.

Learn to create more safety in your body by connecting to the earth. There are several ways to do this. First, you can notice your center of gravity and whether you are holding your energy above your waist (for instance, breathing from your chest and throat, rather than from your diagram). If you react by energetically disappearing from your body when something scares you, it's important to reconnect with the earth. Simply bend your knees and drop your energetic center into your pelvis to shift your energy downward and toward the earth.

You can also imagine energetic cords running down your legs and coming out of the bottom of your central channel or the soles of your feet and into the earth, like the roots of a large tree digging into the soil. Send these cords as deep as possible into the center of the earth. Then, imagine releasing any unwanted energy or feeling nourished and resourced by the earth. This is a powerful way to create more inner sanctuary and connection, making it harder for you to get physically or energetically knocked off your center.

Finally, get outside and walk on the earth. Take your shoes off or get out in nature. Earthing is a thing. You can lie on the grass and feel supported by the earth. Go hug a tree. Notice when you feel too heady and need to be more in your body, then consider practicing these different techniques to find which one resonates and helps you connect within yourself.

RELEASE (PART 2)

The review in RELEASE (Part 2) may have brought up many different aspects of your life that warrant further review and unpacking to help you feel more settled within yourself. This is by no means easy work, which is why the RELEASE step has been broken into two parts.

While each of the seven sections of Part 1 had action steps to address your challenges, two additional strategies follow that you can use at any time to support you in moving through whatever is holding you back to feel more in control of your situation. These powerful tools can help you make important shifts to set you up for the work that is to follow.

RITUAL: Release Challenging Energies

Creating formal rituals helps to symbolically elevate activities that merit deeper intention. The RELEASE step is so important because we often don't realize what we're carrying around unconsciously, the energetic weight of the metaphorical albatross hanging around our necks. We need to know that something is weighing us down and holding us back before we can let go of it. Acknowledging we are finally ready to be done and put down our weights is a helpful way to release them with intention. Recognizing what it has meant to us and thoughtfully setting it aside prevents it from remaining intertwined with our energy and holding us back.

You can create your own release ritual whenever needed, following these basic steps. First, I'll share the process, then I'll provide an example.

- **Challenge:** For each situation, choose an object to represent these aspects of your past (whether it's a belief written on a piece of paper, something from that experience, or anything convenient). Find something to look at, hold, or point to. You can also imagine that person or thing in your mind. State out loud to each individual object that you are now ready to move away from the past. You could even do this with a witness to hold space for you, or on your own.

- **Vision:** Identify what you're moving toward (the ideal future state that is inspiring you to create change). State your desired vision out loud or create an affirmation that speaks to what you wish to create for yourself. The new vision in your mind is the powerful motivator to help you move forward.

- **Objective:** Then, confirm what you are releasing and why. Clearly identify what you no longer wish to hold on to. You can tell that person, object, or experience why you are done with them. Make sure to individually acknowledge each experience, person, or belief that has been unhelpful, if there is more than one, to separate out their specific impacts on you.

- **Lesson:** Claim what you have learned from your experience. Say why you are done with it and are moving forward now.

- **Gratitude:** Be thankful for the experience by acknowledging what it gave you.

- **Release:** With great intention, let it go. Remember the elements and decide how you want to complete your process to bring closure. You could rip up or (carefully) burn the paper, throw it away, set it aside, unwind it in your mind, or watch it dissolve into thin air. Do whatever activity helps you release this energy.

- **Reflect:** Once you have let it go and completed the release, check in with yourself. Do you feel free and lighter? If not, what else do you need? Sometimes, taking a bath can be very cleansing to support a clearing ritual. Do whatever else will help you put your burden down. It's important to notice the sense of liberation and nonattachment.

- **Move Forward:** You are now ready to step into your new vision. Imagine a line right in front of you. See what you want to create ahead of you on the other side of the line, and name it out loud to claim it. Declare that you are moving toward what you want. With focused intention, step over the line into your new future.

- **Acknowledge:** Now, celebrate! Yay! You have just taken a huge step toward unwinding your past so you can move uninhibited toward your future path with energy, excitement, and ease.

Example: You had a horrible boss in your last job and worry that other jobs could be similar. You decide it's time to create a new belief that future opportunities could be better. Here's how you might walk through the process above:

- ¤ Imagine yourself in a dynamic new job with a wonderful manager and mentor.
- ¤ Decide to confront your old boss and tell him everything you didn't have a chance to
- ¤ Imagine your old boss standing across from you.
- ¤ Say out loud: "Beth, you were the worst boss I ever worked for. I wish I quit last year. You were a difficult, overcontrolling micromanager, and I resent how difficult you made my work at [XYZ company]. I wanted to love

that job, but working with you was incredibly stressful and unpleasant."

¤   Now, share the lesson. "After working for you I've learned that, in the future, I will carefully screen any manager to make sure our values and work styles are aligned. I now know I prefer working from home and need more independence and flexibility than I realized, which will factor into any future work I do."

¤   Express your gratitude. "Thank you for teaching me that lesson. I now release you!"

¤   Check in with yourself that you feel lighter. You may choose to physically shake any heaviness off with your hands and push it out of your field.

¤   See that exciting new opportunity and mentor again waiting to welcome you.

¤   Step forward and breathe a huge sigh of relief.

¤   Do that football touchdown celebration dance, because you no longer work for someone you hate ... and know you're moving on to something better!

EXERCISE: Build Boundaries by Understanding Your Triggers

In Part 1, you may have discovered situations that cause you to get defensive, feel uncomfortable, or overreact. This often happens when someone has impinged upon us energetically or reminds us of some aspects of ourselves that we feel uncomfortable with. We often respond on multiple levels: physically in our bodies, mentally through our thoughts and stories in our heads, and emotionally with strong feelings. It's important to explore how all these different aspects hijack our sense of calm.

Looking more closely at how you get activated or triggered lets you begin to change your reactions and create more ease in your life. Setting clear boundaries around what you will and will not tolerate can help you define life on your own terms. Use the table below to identify which challenging situations, words, or people create stress for you.

Noticing *how you react, what you think, and how you feel* in specific types of situations or with certain people will give you important clues about what may be going on, so you can develop more empowering alternative strategies. Go through the prompts in the column headings of the table below to recognize which situations make you susceptible to having your boundaries breached. Noticing these patterns can help you develop constructive new approaches to shift your reactions and mindset to minimize future issues.

	TRIGGERS Which situations, words, or people stress you?	RESPONSES How do you react physiologically (sweating, tightness in chest ...)?	THOUGHTS What messages do you tell yourself? Is there a story or assumption?	EMOTIONS What feelings come up for you (fear, anger, sadness, annoyance)?
1				
2				
3				
4				
5				

Now, review the following prompts to uncover any patterns that you want to become more aware of going forward so you can develop new, more productive approaches that can support you in the future.

- *This reminds me of ...* What similar historical challenges can you recall?

- *Healthy actions I can take are ...* How can you react differently and protect yourself in the future?

- *My positive mindset will be ...* What will you say to yourself to help you return to your center? Which affirming thoughts can reframe your situation so you will feel more in control of your reactions?

- *My learning will include ...* How will you take care of yourself in the future? What might you do differently next time?

Here are some additional practical tips and suggestions to help you center yourself.

- **Notice the Signs:** Pay attention and look for patterns that are your red flags, so you become more aware of these in the future.

- **Minimize Difficult Situations:** Prepare for or avoid occasions that you anticipate may press your hot buttons. Develop effective strategies or responses to counter recurring issues. Go over the situation in advance to mentally review how you will respond if it comes up again.

- **Work through Strong Emotions:** Notice whether you still have a charge when thinking about the situation. If you still feel activated, there may be additional underlying issues to uncover that remain to be addressed. If you still feel anger, resentment, bitterness, jealousy, or any other strong negative emotion, find a way to resolve your underlying need. You may find journaling or talking with someone helpful to uncover what is really going on.

- **Practice Makes Perfect:** New skills take time to develop. Awareness is the first step to creating change and ongoing improvement, and consistently using new behaviors will reinforce them. Just like you would rehearse before making a speech, regularly review those behaviors that you want to build.

- **Breathe and Ground:** When you get knocked off balance, know that you can return to the grounding practices above to center yourself. Make time to reconnect with yourself to reduce reactions whenever you feel you need to take a break.

- **Change the Story:** Create new beliefs to turn negative experiences into opportunities for growth. Incorporate your affirmations and remind yourself of how you want to show up in the future, so you continue to work toward how you want to act and be seen.

Congratulations on doing the deep work of getting to know yourself better! Only through awareness and understanding can you start to shift your experience. You are moving toward gaining more clarity and confidence, and you are just getting started, so keep up the great work!

RECLAIM

TRUST and INTEGRATE
The final step of your INNER WORK brings together all that you have learned to feel more whole.

CHAKRA: Reinforce your HEART chakra to bring deeper connections and love into your life.

COLOR: GREEN or PINK support your heart to heal and expand.

ELEMENT: EARTH can nourish and support you to ground and center yourself.

POWER ANIMAL:
JAGUAR can support you to courageously move through challenges and darkness to emerge fearless.

CRYSTALS:

ROSE QUARTZ is a heart-expanding crystal that encourages love and acceptance.

GREEN AVENTURINE is a nourishing and supportive crystal to expand your positive energy.

TAROT CARDS:

THE CHARIOT represents your inner strength and the application of your will to direct your future. You have more power than you realize.

The STRENGTH card helps you recognize and accept your true wild nature and overcome challenges through inner fortitude and faith.

AFFIRMATION:

"I connect within to reclaim my passion."

STEP 3: RECLAIM

TRUST AND INTEGRATE (PART 1)

Ideally, you are feeling lighter, less encumbered by the weight of the past, and more open to possibility now that you have worked through challenges you identified in the RELEASE step. The RECLAIM step will guide you to fully integrate all aspects of yourself, so you can move forward with intention.

RECLAIM connects you with your sacral chakra, the source of your passion and creativity. You will reflect on what you love and are passionate about. Remember who or what you wanted to be when you grew up? This can reveal inner motivations about your early dreams. While you may no longer wish to be a firefighter, police officer, or veterinarian, your desire to help others could reflect a genuine interest in being of service. Also consider where you spend your time now, since your actions demonstrate what you care most about.

As you look to the future, consider these metaphorical choices for how you might proceed with your path. You could go:

- **Under:** This route entails going deep within to understand what is needed for you to be of service. Like digging a tunnel or going into hibernation, and then emerging with a new perspective, you may need an internalized reflective process to incubate your ideas before choosing how to proceed.

- **Over:** Here, you decide to rise above whatever is standing in your way, by doing the work, getting support, and surpassing any limitations (whether external or self-imposed) to move ahead. Climbing a mountain to the summit can be challenging but worth reaching the view at the top to get a broader perspective. Looking back on what you overcame can help you chart your path forward.

- **Through:** Sometimes, we must push ahead with persistence, like a bull charging at the toreador's red cape. Like pulling back the bow to let the arrow fly straight to its target, a take-no-prisoners approach can make sh*t happen on the path to your purpose. Your focus, commitment, and passion can fuel the pursuit of your dreams.

- **Around:** When you're uncertain where you're going, then any route will do. This path of discovery and exploration follows fortune wherever it takes you. Choosing a more scenic, winding road around the mountain in front of you may lead you to a place you couldn't anticipate.

- **Back:** You may need to return to previous experiences if you didn't learn your lesson the first time. This could entail revisiting prior work, travel, or opportunities that you missed or didn't fully appreciate at the time. This might also mean returning to aspects of yourself or things you loved that you walked away from. The spiral exemplifies this cycle of getting a second chance to revisit something you wanted or being pushed to resolve issues you didn't address earlier.

The diagram below shows that your route from the present starts at the same place but can go in various directions. Each route may eventually lead to a similar outcome, perhaps at a different time ... or not. You can't know. It's simply a matter of your choices, preferences, luck, and timing. Each hero/heroine's journey presents different experiences and lessons, some longer and more arduous than others, depending on the circumstances.

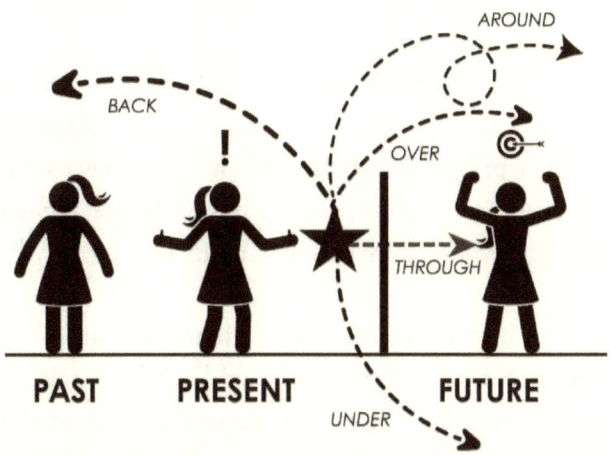

Determine where you want to go from where you are now and where you came from. Will your path take you back, around, over, under, through or beyond?

As I've shared, at various times, I have taken each path with its respective pros and cons. There is no right or wrong choice; just where you are in your personal process and what appeals, invites, or pushes you to move forward.

- - - - - - - -

As you *reclaim* yourself, you will rediscover who you truly are. The real *you*! This knowledge and self-awareness will help you integrate lost parts of yourself to become more whole. You might find and reengage with interests, hobbies, or passions you set aside in the past (whether from fear, judgment, distraction, or prioritizing other activities). You can recognize why you let them go and decide whether to take them back. Who were you then, and why did you choose to let them go? Which judgments were you afraid of? What do you want to reincorporate into your life, and what is meant to be left in the past?

Stay open to this reflection process, as it may surprise you. It's hard to know what this new version of you will look like. Maybe you loved animals or being in nature as a child; now, you could get training or work in these areas or perhaps get a pet, volunteer at an animal shelter, or start gardening more.

At the same time, there is no hard-and-fast rule that who you wanted to be as a child is who you need to be as an adult. Honor yourself to see if previous interests are now complete or ready to resurface with some wisdom for you now. Choose what matters most to you and what to own, so you can feel more whole and integrated.

While you are still and always *you*, it is possible that you are ready to step into a new identity or peel back layers that covered your truth, so it can shine through to be seen and appreciated now by you and others. *You get to just be you—no more faking, hiding, or denying what you care about. It's less about making others happy or caring what they think, and more about owning your truth.*

This starts with recognizing ways you haven't been truthful to yourself. Perhaps fear or insecurity ran the show before, and now you need to rebuild your confidence and start acting with integrity and alignment to walk your talk. As you shift your thoughts and behaviors, you will begin to trust yourself more and new possibilities will emerge.

The example below illustrates how our expectations can get in the way of recognizing who we are and what we care most about. When we come back to ourselves and listen to our hearts, we can follow the breadcrumbs, and the path forward becomes much easier to see and embrace.

CLIENT STORY: Evolutionary Introvert

My client, Ellen, was well-educated, in her thirties, married, and in a new job. She had just decided to end her independent consulting business of ten years to move into a full-time project management position. She had determined the credibility, endorsement, and experience of working for an established company in addition to her project management professional (PMP) certification would enhance her background.

While she thought she had joined a forward-thinking organization aligned with her values, she quickly became disillusioned as she realized the interview process had mischaracterized both the job expectations and how the company operated. Their values were simply window dressing and were not being demonstrated in practice; and Ellen's open, collaborative operating style differed significantly from her boss who was highly political and controlling.

We decided to help her explore other roles at the company within different business lines. After conversations with different managers, she could not find an appealing position and did not want to stay. We revisited her consulting business, which she had enjoyed, appreciating its independence and flexibility. However, Ellen shared some frustration that many clients had not fully valued her contributions.

Upon further reflection, Ellen revealed that she didn't enjoy project management as much as research and writing. This was ironic, as she realized the PMP certification was a practical external marker no longer required for the work she wanted to do. In many ways, it had been keeping her from her real desires, and she was ready to release her attachment to it. In acknowledging her true interests and inner introvert tendencies, she could completely redirect her focus to what she cared most about. We then completely repositioned her role and restructured her consulting offerings toward more of the work she most wanted, and we shifted her pricing model to better reflect her effort and value.

She quickly took on new research and writing projects and pursued a doctorate in public policy, receiving a fellowship grant to operate at a higher level. Not only was Ellen able to retain her freedom and leave undesirable organizational politics behind, but she began stepping into more thought leadership in those areas that were most meaningful to her. Ellen had completely rebranded herself and her work—both how she presented herself and her capabilities to prospective clients, and how she saw and defined herself and her skills. By embracing her true interests, she attracted exciting new projects aligned with her interests, allowing her to do work she loved and make a positive impact for mission-driven organizations.

Ellen later faced some family challenges and lost a close parent. Energy medicine and dream work helped to address some unresolved past issues so she could move forward with more ease. A year later, we reconnected, and I marveled at her continued growth. She was focused on enhancing her personal relationships and was confidently making choices aligned with her truth and values. She no longer felt obligated to conform and perform or make others happy. Ellen is living authentically and doing inspiring work based on her values of community impact, connection, and inclusion.

" I carried hidden and overt expectations from my family, cultures, and society. As a first-generation immigrant, I came to this country in pursuit of a dream education. I grew up in countries where opportunities were limited, especially for someone *like me who liked to push the boundaries of what's possible. The longest career lesson I learned was that, as much as there are hidden expectations, I can decide what to expect of myself. The biggest expectations are the ones I create for myself and the ones I allow others to impose on me. I learned to shape my path based on my values and aspirations, not just on external pressures. I see things now more in nuances, being comfortable in the gray.* **"**

—Ellen

You can't really know where you're going until you know where you've been.

—Maya Angelou

Resistance Is Futile

I've seen so many clients deny what they want most, out of fear that they won't be able to make it happen or be successful at what they love. Don't let this be you! Your work is to stop trying to ignore, deny, or fight who you are. While you can keep pushing away what you're drawn to, why wouldn't you move toward what you enjoy, to streamline the direction to your true path?

Don't limit your possibilities. The fields with strict training requirements and background criteria are few and far between. Rocket scientists are typically engineers, but if astronautics fascinates you, explore other capacities in that field. Not everyone has the optimal physical build to be a prima ballerina or professional footballer, but you could pursue closely related work to these interests (for instance, at the amateur level or through organizations involved with those activities). Local sports leagues, dance performances, or dance companies offer ways to become involved, even if not for your day job. Think outside the box to overcome perceived limitations or constraints.

In moving forward, you might get sidelined or delayed and learn important lessons along the way; however, know you will eventually be led to what you are meant to do, so you can be yourself.

- - - - - - - -

Self-acceptance comes from knowing you are exactly where you are meant to be right now. You are unique, and it's counterproductive to try to be something that you're not. Besides, everyone else is taken. If you slow down and drop into inner stillness, consider how being yourself feels. Can you hear and listen to the stirrings of your heart and soul? This is your opportunity to define success and fulfillment on your terms, to stop feeling frustrated that you haven't achieved enough or done as much as (or more than) your peers or family.

In this chapter, you will consider how to find yourself by accepting your unique gifts, those aspects of yourself that are your secret sauce, your warrior's powers. It's time for you to play your own game and make your own rules.

Here are some elements to put in place to help you move forward on your own terms.

Discover and Do Your Research

To uncover your soul path, you must learn as much as possible about yourself (what you do and don't like) and what opportunities are available. You need to do your homework (or growth work, if that sounds more enjoyable). Gather information as you go, and learn by doing, to get real experience in the areas that fascinate you.

I have seen students make assumptions about different jobs without doing their due diligence. When questioned about position details, they didn't know or weren't sure. Why? Because they hadn't done their homework. Don't guess what something is like or assume you know what it will be until you begin reality testing; otherwise, you are just pie-in-the-sky. Gather information through conversations, read about your interests, and pursue areas that appeal to you. Follow the breadcrumbs wherever they lead you.

Read an article about a company doing something interesting, then explore their website to learn more about their work; this might redirect you to other industry articles. Before you know it, you've uncovered a new area that fascinates you. Then, you could formulate questions to learn more, reach out through LinkedIn to connect with contacts doing that work, attend an industry event, or read a book to uncover more information.

These are just examples of one approach among many. There is no right way to learn, only your way. You are more likely to be interested in those things that interest you! Sharing what you really care about will drive more engagement than compulsory updates or interactions with no heart that you feel obligated to do. The performative becomes perfunctory. You want to find what is inspiring.

Go down the rabbit hole and discover whatever fascinates you! Going through your process will uncover more insight. Analyze what you find to see what patterns emerge, then use these themes to develop hypotheses about where to focus. You are an explorer following a treasure map and trying to discover the pot of gold, but some of the clues may be hidden.

You won't know what this will reveal until you go follow Alice to Wonderland. While it might seem like a waste of time to get distracted by every shiny new object, you can always give yourself parameters if you're worried about getting off track. For instance, spend one hour (or thirty minutes) researching and reading articles that interest you, then reflect in your journal about what you observed and why it interested you. Or, if you prefer engaging directly, reach out to five people through LinkedIn, recognizing that only two might respond, then schedule calls with them the following week.

Jane, an experienced professional who had never been unemployed, was in between jobs and trying to make a career pivot but was struggling with open-ended time. She would distract herself with things to do around the house and would get stuck in her head. She found it hard to focus and needed some structure but knew that she would get engaged once she got started. We identified five activities she could do every day (reaching out on LinkedIn, doing research, calling a friend, attending an event, searching online job boards) and designed a weekly schedule with time blocks so Jane always had somewhere to go or something to do. This helped her feel productive, so she could just get started and move out of her comfort zone.

Uncover New Opportunities

Consider the impact you want to make in the world. If that feels too heady, how would you like to feel? How can you bring all your life experiences together to support you going forward? Go crazy and brainstorm on this a bit. Consider writing down what comes up for you as you explore the following prompts that are inviting you to think outside the box. Are new skills needed for opportunities you want to pursue to broaden your knowledge and position you for the future? Can you mix and match things you've already done but apply them in new ways?

You may wish to revisit the Life Work Assessment exercise from Step 1: REALIZE to give you a sense of your vision (what you want to create in the world) and your values (what you care about). *Has anything changed or shifted* since you let go of old habits, patterns, behaviors, or thoughts (from Step 2: RELEASE)?

Ask what resonates with you now and where you want to put your energy and focus. Research your interests, and translate your existing experience into new ways of being. If you realize you need more experience, figure out how to get it. How might you experiment and take risks? How willing are you to try new things? Can you explore projects outside of or within your current full-time work commitments, such as volunteering, taking on some special initiative, or pursuing something independently?

Who could you connect with or learn from? How can you get more exposure to things that interest you? Is there someone you can talk with or be mentored by, or a class, course, or training program you can take? How much preparation do you need, or can you just jump in and start acting right away? Assess your own comfort level, and build your confidence through learning and experience.

PRACTICE: Learn by Doing to Discover Your Interests

Actions speak louder than words, and information is power. The best way to discover what you enjoy is by gaining actual experience and gathering information about areas that fascinate you; otherwise, your decisions will be based on pure hypothesis and speculation.

What is one step you can take now to move forward with your interests and vision? What information or conversations do you need to have to get more clarity? Here are a few ideas to get you started. Of the five ideas below, choose your top three to focus on.

- **Research:** Gather information by reading articles and websites to see what interests you. Write about your discoveries and see where your fascination guides you. Learn more about what you like, and uncover things you didn't know, to decide where to direct your focus next.

- **Real Experience:** Is there a project you could take on, whether through an existing job or independently, that would help you to learn more about the areas you are interested in? You can design your own experiments to help you develop your skills. Be creative if you can't do exactly what you want; find related things that might expose you to similar opportunities.

- **Informational Interviews:** Who can you speak with to learn more from? Connect with others with the intention of gathering insight and learning from diverse perspectives to inform your choices, not just to get a job. These individuals could be classmates, friends of friends, referrals from teachers or colleagues, someone you don't know but you read about in an article, or someone you met through an event or identified through LinkedIn. Your goal here is to engage with the spirit of learning and build a relationship.

  ¤ Keep in mind that it's much easier to make a meaningful connection when you have a legitimate desire to learn, so offer a compelling reason why you wish to speak with them. Most people love to talk about what they do, if someone appears to have some knowledge and seems genuinely interested.

  ¤ Try to make a compelling ask, explaining your interest and why you're reaching out. Offer to share information with them to create a mutually beneficial conversation.

  ¤ Warm introductions or referrals can also be helpful, and many busy people will prioritize references from those they know.

  ¤ If you don't hear back or receive a response to your outreach, be patient and persistent with follow-up. It can often take several times to get someone's attention, so don't take it personally if you don't hear back.

- **Listen:** Are there podcasts, YouTube videos, TED Talks, lectures, or events that might have information about your interests? Identify one or more sources you can listen to this week.

- **Hobbies:** Reconnect with your passions. Join a club, take a class (in person or online), or find a local meetup. Pick up something you may have set aside (a craft activity, project, or other interest), and make time to play and see how that feels. In *The Artist's Way*, an inspiring book for creatives and creators, author Julia Cameron recommends scheduling a weekly "artist date" to explore your interests. This is a wonderful way to give yourself permission to do something creative for the sake of doing it, rather than to produce an outcome.

Choose actions that are manageable and doable. Select activities that you know you will complete, to give you a sense of accomplishment. If you want a challenge, set a stretch goal just beyond your comfort zone. For instance, could you reach out to three people to ask about their work and spend one hour this week to explore more? Or, could you start asking friends to recommend people you could speak to in your area of interest?

Try doing something that scares you a little, or makes you uncomfortable, to see how it feels. Taking a step toward what you want will give you more insight and help you gain practical experience to make you more knowledgeable about what you do and don't like.

CHECK-IN: Define Your Work and Lifestyle

The Life Work Assessment exercise (in Step 1: REALIZE) helped you evaluate how you like to work. Consider whether anything has shifted as your self-awareness and process have evolved. Reflect on the following questions to develop more clarity on what you need and want in how you live and work.

- **Lifestyle:** Do you prefer flexibility or structure? Do you see yourself working from home, being completely virtual and remote, or would you prefer to be in an office, do something hybrid, or be outdoors without any office? Are you an introvert, needing lots of quiet or private time, or are you more extroverted, needing to be around people to feel energized?

- **Work Style:** Would you like to be independent and self-sufficient in your work, or would you benefit from having a manager and team to collaborate with? Do you want to have structure and training, or learn on the job or as you go, in a more ad hoc, unstructured fashion? Is it appealing to be a big fish in a small pond, or a small fish in a big pond? How much feedback do you need on your work? Are you a team person or would you prefer to be a solo performer?

Clarifying what you like and don't like helps you uncover the types of work best suited to your preferences and opportunities that align with your values and desired operating style. Keep directing your energy toward those specific opportunities that appeal most to you. Continue revealing what most aligns with your desires.

EXERCISE: Choose Three Priorities

In clarifying your needs and interests, you can focus even more. Are you ready to choose a direction to pursue now? Remember, you can easily change your focus as you learn more; however, start by choosing the area you want to prioritize right now.

Identify your three most exciting interests to explore further. You can narrow your choices to your top two to make your process even easier, though three choices will give you a nice variety of options.

A helpful rule of thumb is to focus on what brings you joy, and how you would ideally want to spend your time. Shift your mindset from what you should be doing (things that you are good at and *like* enough) to what lights you up (passions that you *love*). Remember, being good at something doesn't mean you have to do it just because it comes easily to you. You are more likely to enjoy and get more out of doing what you are truly interested in.

Questions to ask yourself are:

- Given a choice, how do you spend your free time? Why? What do you like to do most?

- What is it about these activities that brings you joy?

- Could you translate elements of those things you love into your work, or would you prefer to keep them as hobbies or personal interests?

Imagine your *ideal day*, from the moment you wake up in the morning until when you go to sleep. How are you spending your time? What are you doing? How do you feel? Where do you live? Who are you interacting with? Ask yourself these questions in the present tense, as if they are happening to you right now.

Remember, you get to define your most critical priorities. Review how you spend your time now (consider your balance pie chart allocations from Step 1: REALIZE) to align your actions more with your priorities. What were those nonnegotiable items for you? These tell you what truly matters.

Revisit these important areas: money, flexibility and freedom, structure, culture, learning, growth, challenge, contribution, justice, and your/the environment. Remind yourself what is essential for you to have, and what you desire in and from your life and work. Are there things that you absolutely cannot tolerate? Use these criteria to decide where you will focus.

RECLAIM (PART 2)

Transformation and uncertainty go hand in hand as we undergo change and don't know what, how, or where things will evolve. Learning to be comfortable navigating the unknown is an important skill to master. This section offers suggestions for how to address challenges we may face and get support to move toward more trust and inner knowing.

•

Overcoming Fear of Change

Since our biological wiring wants to control our environment, we find change scary because we crave consistency. We prefer the status quo, staying where we are and doing what we know, even if we're unhappy or uncomfortable. For many of us, inertia is the default—choosing comfort rather than venturing into the unknown. ("The devil you know is better than the devil you don't.") We prefer safety and certainty over change and unpredictability.

Expecting to face resistance (both internal and external) can help us persist despite strong emotions or reactions that may try to hold us back. We've reviewed many of the ways we protect ourselves or become defensive in Step 2: RELEASE; now, we will look at how outside influences can impact us.

The Golden Goose

While you may not value your gifts, you may be a goose who lays golden eggs for others. You may have heard of "golden handcuffs," when organizations lock in executives and valuable employees for extended periods of time with highly lucrative perquisites from higher compensation to options and other benefits intended to keep them tied to the organization for a longer period. There is a payoff for staying, while leaving has a penalty. There are multiple ways we can become trapped in roles imposed by others or of our own making.

Some people focus on a "number" they want to hit to reach a specific financial income target. After reaching this milestone, the goalpost may move again, extending their work instead of pursuing their own interests. Why? To retain credibility, take care of others, to retain their work identity, because "it's the right thing to do," or any other rationale.

We always have choices, and it can be helpful to explore whether you may be sacrificing yourself or putting up barriers to your happiness without realizing it. Review the reasoning for your decisions to make sure you aren't avoiding something, someone, or difficult conversations you should be having with yourself or others. The story below illustrates an example.

A startup founder, Joe, approached me for mentoring. He wanted to leave his corporate job to launch the early-stage technology business he was building on evenings and weekends as a side hustle. Since his entire family (spouse and parents) depended on him to support them financially as the primary breadwinner, he couldn't figure out how to leave his steady job and paycheck to pursue his vision of running the business full time.

Joe felt stuck and was burned-out in his job, but without dedicating time to his startup, he couldn't find funding to get it off the ground. It required a big risk to believe in himself, leave the full-time job, and commit to his dream. His difficult choice was between his own health, realizing his vision, and taking care of those he cared for and about. He was the "cash cow" others relied upon to fund their lives, yet no one would benefit if he got sick. Brave and difficult conversations were needed with his family to explore what might need to shift.

Sometimes, there aren't easy answers, and compromises may be needed. Starting a new business or making any professional change, like any important endeavor, requires commitment, focus, and difficult choices. When decisions have implications for others, you can look for a way forward that works for all parties while still taking your own needs into account.

Navigating your impact on others can be challenging, yet it is necessary to do your work in the world. While you can take others along on your journey, they may resist and not want you to change. You may discover that different people are needed to support you at different stages of your journey. As you become more of your true self, some people you previously relied upon may begin to fall away as you change, which is also part of the growth process.

EXERCISE: Build Your Dream Team

While you walk your path alone, it can be nice to have company along the way. Relationships provide powerful leverage to help you find what you want (six degrees of separation connect you to anyone). Focus more on quality than quantity, having fewer well-connected individuals can be more powerful than many loose connections.

Build a fan base and a group of individuals to surround yourself with for input, advice, mentorship, feedback, and direction. Choose people who will support you with unbiased perspectives and inspire you as you move into your new identity. These may be friends, family, teachers, mentors, role models, coaches, guides, groups, or a chosen soul family, tribe, or community.

You want to find folks with your best interests in mind, not their own, who can listen and hold space for your exploration without trying to direct or point you toward things that may not make sense for you. Look for enthusiasm and love, not doubt and criticism—those who won't feel threatened by your changing, leveling up, and going after what you want.

Who can you rely upon to understand and encourage the changes you are making? Notice who listens to you and your needs without trying to project their own stuff onto you. Who do you trust and feel safe sharing vulnerable parts of yourself with? Who has your back and will give you honest, impartial feedback?

Who have you seen, or would you like to know, who has achieved the success you desire? Look for positive examples in friends, classmates, media (leaders, celebrities or influencers), or articles. Notice who you feel drawn to, and why. A role model is someone you admire and who inspires you. Why? What aspects of their life and work would you like to emulate? We often already have the qualities we are drawn to, though they may not be fully expressed yet. Others often mirror hidden aspects of ourselves we may not own or fully allow.

Where and how will you find them? Many individuals may already be within your extended network. If you are looking to create new relationships, you can do virtual outreach through LinkedIn, on other social media channels or online events, or by meeting people in person through personal connections, meetups, your local coworking space, conferences, or industry forums. Develop rapport with those in your field of focus who can help you, provide referrals, and make recommendations about different companies or areas to consider (friends of friends can be helpful resources). Decide which approach makes the most sense for your style.

Your dream team should include different types of people, like a board of advisors, for input and support in multiple areas. Who could give you advice on strategy, marketing, health, mindset, spiritual fulfillment, or growth? Find those you respect, with more experience in what you wish to do. Peers facing similar challenges can be helpful resources. Even those with no background in your area of interest who love you can offer unconditional support.

Sometimes, close friends or family may have personal biases; for instance, the desire for you to stay the same in whatever "role" you have played. When those you love show resistance to your changes, consider what and how to share with them. Protect and keep your process to yourself until you feel confident and safe to share more widely. Find unbiased resources who truly have your best interests at heart.

Perfect is the enemy of good.
—Voltaire

The Myth of Perfection

Let's dispel two flawed assumptions. First, there is not only one perfect job, career, or calling for you; multiple paths are possible. Second, you do not need to do or get everything right or be perfect; you are fantastic as you are. Seeking perfection creates unnecessary pressure when all you need to focus on is your next best choice, and then go from there. Should your direction not feel right, then switch; you can go backward, sideways, or somewhere else.

Follow your passions and interests to expand your knowledge and build connections to what you care about. This is how to uncover exciting opportunities you can't even imagine at this moment. Redirect your energy toward doing what is aligned with who you are and what you want and need in your life now. There are multiple avenues that could bring fulfillment and meaning to your life and work, so choose which alternative makes the most sense to pursue now—at this point in your life, experience, age, stage, place where you live, and your family obligations.

Certain jobs require specific backgrounds to demonstrate knowledge or meet state and local licensing requirements, and you must meet those criteria for that type of work to comply with the regulations. However, obtaining an advanced degree does not guarantee ease in switching careers. You must do the work—the hard work of educating yourself about your desired industry and opportunities, building your network, learning the lingo, and positioning your background. Most career paths involve these practical steps to develop your confidence and credibility and show others you have what it takes to succeed. Entering any new area involves learning as much as possible about it.

Competence doesn't happen overnight, but through doing, learning, assessing, and integrating. Reading books gives you information, but practical experiences become wisdom. Certificates and training can introduce new skills, so discover how to become knowledgeable in your focus area.

Dealing with Imposter Syndrome

Even experienced professionals can doubt themselves and their credibility, so don't expect to know everything right away when you are moving into something new. What's most important is that you learn to trust and have confidence in yourself. When you know what you want, believe in yourself, can articulate your value, and persevere in the face of challenges, then you will find the right opportunities.

This book is intended to help you let go of your fears, stand in your power, and message your value. I'd like to address some specific issues that I know many individuals worry about, so you have some additional perspective.

How to address your concerns? Turn your liabilities into assets and develop counters for any perceived weaknesses. These are three common issues that arise. While you may worry that you don't measure up in some way, it's simply not true. Your skills are valuable, and you have a contribution to make. Your goal is to find the organizations, companies, or clients that need what you have to offer.

- **Work Experience Gaps:** *How to address being out of the work force for over six months (due to a layoff, a health issue, or family matters)?* Circumstances may have been beyond your control, and you made a choice in how you managed your situation. Decide how best to succinctly convey what happened and how you responded. Consider the communications channel in determining how much to share.

   Discuss how you used the time productively in some capacity to turn your circumstances into a lesson in resiliency. For example, an unexpected personal challenge required you to manage family matters which kept you from full-time work. However, during this time, you employed organizational skills in caring for an elderly parent and managing their affairs. You could summarize that period as family leave when presenting yourself.

- **Age:** *Believe you are too old, or too young and inexperienced?* Either belief can (and will) hold you back, and neither is completely true. Some companies do prefer younger professionals, while others value wisdom and impact. Seek out organizations where your skills, experience, and values are a fit. Since your age is a fact that can be easily validated, there is no value in lying or dissembling. You may initially de-emphasize your age by not referencing your year of graduation, though this information will likely be revealed eventually. Company employment checks often confirm dates, so honesty is the best policy. Know and articulate your value, experience, and contribution when communicating with others.

Early career starters, and those moving to or from a different country, benefit from conveying energy, competence, and enthusiasm and emphasizing their ability to bridge any perceived background gap through relevant experiences. Some organizations may make age-based hiring assumptions (whether legal or not), preferring junior staff for entry-level roles. Experienced, older professionals are more likely to find opportunities through their networks or organizations with diverse workforces that value maturity and expertise, which are important strengths to highlight.

Insurance and financial advisory businesses do hire experienced career switchers from other backgrounds; however, these roles often have low base salaries, if not completely commission-based, and require strong sales and relationship-building skills. Organizations most want employees who can make an impact through meaningful contributions. You are bringing a full package, and your age (whatever number) is just one variable. Look for the best fit between your background and expectations (around compensation, title, level, flexibility, and other factors).

- **Training:** *Is an additional degree or certification needed to enter a new field?* This depends on your level of knowledge, your confidence, and the job requirements for roles you are pursuing. Sadly, no education or certificate guarantees a job in any field—that is a fallacy. Opportunities result from many factors (economic conditions, background, fit, connections, etc.). Advanced training can provide additional credibility, build new skills, provide exposure to new opportunities, and expand one's network—which are all valuable. Building relationships; gaining relevant experience; and strengthening your ability to message and communicate your interests, unique perspectives, and contributions are arguably more important when moving to a new area.

I know many individuals who built their skills into successful careers by learning on the job. Research and validate that a specific degree or training is a requirement before you decide to make that costly investment. While not all jobs require a college degree, having relevant work experience is often a priority and will help you move. Just like driving a new car before buying it, road testing can provide information before fully committing to anything. Understand the lingo of your new field and translate your related skills to make a compelling case that you currently have (or can learn) what's needed. Research can prevent you from pursuing a degree only to discover you don't like the field or need that training for what you ultimately want.

If you still struggle with insecurity and perfectionism, revisit the work in Step 2: RELEASE around your beliefs. Inner compassion and confidence are important to move through risk and uncertainty. Learn to trust your ability to face whatever challenges present themselves, knowing that you have made it this far already and will learn and grow from every experience.

RITUAL: Self-Care Practices

Transformation can bring up a lot of uncertainty as one's identity, perspective, experiences, values, and priorities change. It's important to have personal strategies to help you center and return to your vision, so you don't get distracted or pushed off course by minor setbacks or the emotional vicissitudes of life.

Here are some ideas to support you in taking care of yourself.

Choose two or more of the activities below when you feel challenged, ambivalent, or less than optimistic about your path.

- **Visualization:** Bring yourself back to your original vision of the life and work you are creating. Remind yourself how you want to feel in the life you are creating. Give yourself five to ten minutes (or more) to immerse yourself in those juicy feelings of excitement and possibility. If you don't feel inspired, ask yourself what is missing, so that you can create a more compelling new vision that motivates you to move forward.

- **Affirmations:** Choose a statement to remind you of what you are creating and how you want to feel. Either use one included in each step's reference overview or create your own using positive statements that remind you of who you are. As soon as you notice any resistance to what you're doing or challenging feelings (such as negativity or despair), call it out, and remember your positive belief to turn around your thoughts.

- **Meditate:** Take a moment to pause and notice your breath, focusing on the inhale and exhale. Consider setting a timer or doing a guided meditation (you can find these through Spotify, Insight Timer, or other mindfulness apps) for five minutes or more. There are many types of meditation approaches. Find what works best for you. Notice your thoughts without attaching to them. Let them pass like clouds in the sky, so you can avoid getting bogged down in over analysis. Meditation can prevent your doubts from overwhelming you or becoming critical self-talk.

- **Move or Walk:** Take a break when you feel stuck or frustrated and stop what you're doing. Get outside or put on some music and move your body. Get away from where you are to shift your frame of reference and get a new perspective. Maybe grab some tea, do some sit-ups, call a friend, or take a walk around the block.

- **Act:** When you feel uncertain, just do something that will move you forward. Take one manageable action that you can feel good about. Stay focused on what you can achieve by taking small steps over time. Resist the desire to set unrealistic goals or beat yourself up for not doing more. Think about ways to leverage your current experiences or seek new experiences, through part-time or volunteer work, to build your skills.

- **Journal:** Writing is a powerful way to release pent-up thoughts and spark your creativity. When you feel overwhelmed, write down what's going on to get it out of your mind and onto the page where you can leave it. Free association can help you tap into whatever is coming up for you by following your stream of consciousness. This can be a daily practice (Julia Cameron's Morning Pages exercise from *The Artist's Way* is one approach to consider) at any time of the day or whenever you need to create a change in your approach.

- **Plan:** Having a strategy can put your mind at ease by establishing resources to support you over time. Making significant changes can take longer than you expect. Do you have enough money in savings to hold you over? If not, where could you cut back, or what steps can you take to get some relief? Conserve your energy and money as much as possible to build a buffer and create more resilience. You will be most effective when making changes from a place of relative stability versus crisis.

- **Call/Connect:** Find a friend, mentor, helpful advisor, or other support buddy to listen to your fears or challenges and encourage you to keep going. Consider groups or programs that offer guidance, so you can connect with others facing similar challenges. This is where working with a coach can offer consistency, accountability, perspective, and positivity.

- **Limit:** Reduce your consumption of social media sources that bring you down or cause you to compare yourself in critical ways with others. If you find that you have certain addictive tendencies (around food, drugs, shopping, or online activities), develop strategies to minimize your access to these potentially detrimental activities. Consciously choose which outside influences you let into your experience by surrounding yourself with as much positivity and inspiration as possible. Notice what motivates you versus what stresses you out, and focus on the former, not the latter.

- **Notice:** Be aware of your reactions to your situations and experiences. Fear of change is real. It's not uncommon to undergo an existential crisis when facing a major life transition. Realize that any resistance may be natural, unless it continues to be reactive. Some symptoms that you may be feeling uncomfortable and need more support are initiating fights, running away from challenges, feeling frozen or stuck, or overfocusing on others at your own expense. The best way to address these is by *feeling and dealing*. Don't avoid whatever issues are coming up to the surface; they are arising to be healed and addressed.

- **Support:** You don't have to go through changes on your own, as much as you may want to. Sometimes, professional input or guidance from someone more experienced in holding space for challenges (like a professional coach, spiritual counselor, or psychotherapist) can be helpful.

- **Patience:** In recognizing that change takes time, be gentle with yourself, and manage your process with realism and practicality. Don't put unnecessary pressure on yourself by setting unrealistic or overly ambitious deadlines, unless you believe this will motivate you to move forward. In many cases, setting unreasonable expectations can be disheartening as you realize that more time may be needed to move in a new direction.

- **Grace:** Be open to synchronicities and possibilities. Remember to find gratitude. Transformation often involves lots of ups and downs—good days and more challenging ones. Celebrate the successes and remind yourself of how you are making progress.

Honor and take exquisite care of yourself as you go through your growth process. As you identify unhelpful thoughts that are getting in your way, consider how to shift your mindset from self-critical, negative beliefs to positive, empowering thoughts. Remember the tools above and know that you have many ways that you can deal with challenges that arise. Your strong, beautiful heart is here to support you and love you up. You got this!

PHASE 2: INTERPERSONAL WORK

REFRAME

AFFIRM and SHARE
Begin your INTERPERSONAL WORK. Articulate what you are creating and clearly communicate to others.

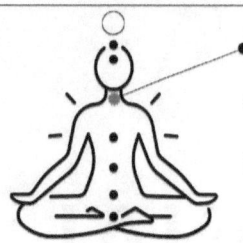

CHAKRA: Use your THROAT chakra to access your voice and speak your truth

COLOR: TURQUOISE to create more ease as you start to share your experience.

ELEMENT: Consider the lightness and spaciousness of AIR to connect with your breath.

POWER ANIMAL:
Let the BLUE JAY encourage you to be authentic and speak your truth.

CRYSTALS:

TURQUOISE grounds you in your unique self-expression

LARIMAR brings brightness and clarity to your wisdom and truth.

TAROT CARDS:

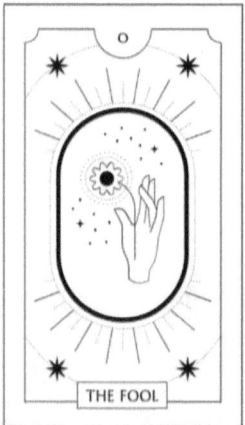

THE FOOL card symbolizes new beginnings. Are you ready to start over with a fresh perspective?

Receive encouragement from the HERMIT card to go within. Contemplate higher wisdom and knowledge.

AFFIRMATION:

"I thoughtfully speak my truth, choosing what, where, how and with whom I share my story."

STEP 4: REFRAME

AFFIRM AND SHARE

It's time to rewrite the old scripts and start telling yourself and the world a new narrative. The REFRAME step is about owning and speaking your truth. Connect with your throat chakra, the source of your voice. Here, your goal will be to notice and replace old beliefs with the new story you are writing now. You are creating a new version of yourself, redefining the rules.

Observe how you speak to others and yourself. Do you use positive language to talk about yourself and the person you want to be? Notice how, when, and where you refer to who or how you were in the past. While that old identity is part of who you are, reaffirm your conscious decision to evolve beyond it.

Staying attached to the past makes it harder to step into your future and desired destiny. Those looking to create change who define and communicate their past identity (focusing on where they worked, what they did, and their former job titles) are creating a disconnect for themselves and others. Choose to communicate who you are becoming and who you want to be, not who you were before. Mixed messages are subtle, often unconscious indications of being stuck and attached to the past. Building confidence in your ability will help you become less ambivalent about releasing your old identity.

The following story demonstrates a successful transition to

a completely new career by an established and experienced professional, highlighting some of the opportunities and challenges of undergoing a major change.

CLIENT STORY: Leadership Fulfillment

Early in her career, Kimberly had a long and successful run in the media. Now, a mother of two in her fifties, she had already made the transition from being a recognized and highly awarded broadcast journalist to working in a new role at a digital media organization. She was now pursuing an exciting new project idea but wasn't getting the traction or resources she had hoped for in her current organization. We decided to explore what was needed to make it take off, either where she was or at another company that could support her ambitious initiative.

During Kimberly's review of her strengths, interests, values, and personal and professional situations, we uncovered that, while she was excited about her project concept, she was also interested in having a leadership role doing meaningful work. At this stage, she wanted to lead and manage a team, make a positive impact, and be recognized for her skills and expertise. It soon became clear that she was not going to get those opportunities in her large organization, so she negotiated her exit.

Once she released the attachment to her project concept, she began to explore multiple new possibilities which surfaced as she expanded her network beyond the media industry. A completely different career path outside of, but adjacent to, the media sector emerged. Over several months, she explored multiple options and ultimately identified a dynamic company that aligned with her values and was seeking a leader with her skills and expertise. It turned out to be a perfect match with what she was looking for: an executive role in a high-growth business building and mentoring a young team.

Kimberly was able to successfully transition into a strategic communications leadership role that offered her the opportunity to scale a business with significant upside potential in terms of her compensation and business development opportunities—key elements she was looking for at this stage in her career.

Her patience and persistence had enabled her to find exactly the environment where she could excel and feel valued. Within three years after successfully growing her division, she was promoted to the C-suite to support the company's continued growth and expansion.

" Don't be afraid to take risks. I'm proud of the risks I've taken in my career, but wish I were less risk averse throughout my twenties and thirties. Also, while hard work is critical, I wish I spent more time networking and developing professional relationships. Too often, I was the last person to leave the newsroom, so consumed with getting the job exactly right that I missed chances to connect. I wish I had focused years earlier on what I wanted in a role and less on the exact role/title/position. Had I done that work, I would have had an easier time making the shift from media and likely would have pursued a leadership role in an entrepreneurial setting earlier. "

—Kimberly

Reposition Yourself

You have been creating a new way of looking at the world, centered on your truth. While I've shared these principles before, they are worth repeating. These are important ways to reinforce the belief that something new is possible.

- **Mindset:** *Are you prepared to put yourself out there?* Embarking on any journey is an act of courage. It takes incredible inner strength and resilience to let go of expectations to make room for possibility. Once you surrender and allow new things to unfold, many new and exciting opportunities will be revealed. It's important to stay positive, even while moving through uncertainty. In short, mindset matters! Keeping your bigger vision in mind will help you weather the storms and challenging aspects of any job search or career-change process. It can help you remember your goals, even if you're working just to pay the bills.

    You are playing the long game, creating the life and work of your dreams. So be in it to win it; stop competing and comparing yourself to others and start doing your own thing. Consistently reconnect to your belief in yourself. Find enthusiasm for your work and process. Build your confidence and belief in yourself by expanding your knowledge. Even without something tangible to point to right now, research and exploration will uncover more. Know you are getting closer to what you want. Trust what makes you unique and believe your efforts will pay off and be rewarded.

- **Center:** *Are you coming from a place of wholeness?* Find and connect to your truth within. Start to understand your needs by listening to and trusting your inner guidance and intuition. Get clear on your intentions and commit to your path as a priority. Practice following your instincts and preferences. For instance, if you want to go in a certain direction, or select a type of food that appeals to you, or wear a particular shirt, say *yes* to yourself. Keep reinforcing your needs and belief in yourself.

Following your intuition reinforces that muscle and will help you feel comfortable using it more. Your confidence will grow as your choices are guided by what matters to you. Learn to say *no* to things that are not aligned with what you want to do. Stay clearly focused on your goals and create boundaries for what doesn't support you.

- **Message:** *How do you describe what you want?* Learn to ask for what you need, and thoughtfully communicate with others. Be clear on what makes you unique and interesting—your distinct differentiators. This could include explaining your skills, translating your experience for the opportunity you are seeking, and describing your qualifications.

  Your exploration process will include uncertainty as you may not yet know exactly what you want to do. This is okay. As you gather more information and focus on your goals, it will become easier to share what you are exploring and why. Let others know how they can help you. Have clear "calls to action" and "asks" as you engage with others, so people understand what you are looking for and can support you.

  As you expand your network, be selective. You don't need to tell everyone everything all the time. Decide what you want to share with whom, and when, as you find your *voice*. Your work is learning how to explain your unique contribution and understanding the area you are targeting so you can speak the lingo.

Note: This guide does not explicitly review how to update your résumé or LinkedIn profile, since other resources are available to support this process. Your focus should result from clearly defining what you want. Based on your goals, you can uncover relevant keywords (also known as "#" or hashtags) and customize your experience and background to jobs you apply for. Encoding the right lingo in all communications helps you connect with your audiences. Focus on three to five of the most important elements of your background for any job to explain your ability and make a positive impact. Additional resources and inspiration are available through my website, newsletter and blog (at www.growthwarrior.co).

- **Market:** *Who is your ideal audience?* Multiple individuals can support you as you pursue your path, from those doing work you are interested in now, to hiring managers and those with different perspectives. Understand the audience you are communicating with to adapt your message accordingly to what they need and want to know. Research how best to grow your network and build relationships to support you in the future. Approach any conversation with a new connection with curiosity, to learn more about them and what they do. Remember to find mutual benefit—how you both might support each other—rather than focusing exclusively on your own goals and what's in it for *you*.

  Approach conversations to learn more about a role, industry, or company informally, with the goal of gathering information. Share your interest in learning more with openness and enthusiasm. Approach outreach to potential employers or applying for positions by being fully prepared and understanding their needs. While the information gathering and initial outreach process can generate interest in working at a company, don't expect that outcome from one initial conversation. Relationships should be cultivated over time. Approach each discussion by keeping the other person's needs and perspective in mind. Find the balance between getting their input for perspective, sharing your interest, and describing your background so they can share more information.

- **Marketing:** *How to put yourself out there?* There are many ways to position yourself as you start pursuing your ideal opportunities. Marketing can feel so salesy and aggressive, so reframe it as relationship building, or the *"fine art of telling people* *what they want to hear,"* a subtler way of actively promoting yourself. Applying directly for jobs online is only one route to employment and is mostly best for entry-level or standardized roles. More experienced leaders (anyone with over ten years of experience), or those looking to switch careers, may need to uncover "hidden" jobs (those not always actively advertised) by working through their network or pursuing nontraditional routes. It's possible to network into opportunities or find meaningful work through relationship building over time.

Connect with others and find the approaches that work for your personality. Here are some ideas based on different styles and personality types.

- Outgoing extroverts who like to socialize should attend in-person events and meet people for coffee or drinks.

- Introverts can do research online or write articles to share their distinct points of view.

- Creatives can leverage social media to communicate value or explore dedicated creative forums.

- Techies can analyze the data and draw conclusions, then share their findings.

- Pet owners can schmooze at the dog park.

- Jocks and athletic types might find more success at their local gym.

There's no one single way to uncover the information you need or connect with others. Find something that gets you engaged and inspired to share your point of view. *Your goals are to get yourself out there; build relationships; and let others know who you are, what you do, and why they might want to work with you.*

Note: While executive recruiters and headhunters can be helpful for senior job placement, they work for the employers who hire them, not you. Building relationships within a broader network is important to get on people's radar, but don't expect recruiters to help you unless your experience is an exact match for a specific position they are prospecting for. Their goal is to fill spots they are working on, so your needs may not necessarily be aligned.

CHECK-IN: Leverage Where You Are Now

To decide where you want to go, start where you are now. *Learn more about what interests you right now!* Below are multiple options that can help you grow beyond what you're doing now.

- **Stay Where You Are:** Make your current work work for you. Explore how you might navigate a change to a new role or find opportunities within your existing organization. Could you work on a key project or committee, or build your network more broadly? Find a more senior mentor within your organization to explore opportunities at your company. Cultivate advocates across your industry who can encourage and support you.

- **Work Part Time:** Could you start freelancing, consulting, or taking on smaller projects to gain experience in the area you're interested in? Temporary work allows you to earn an income while still having time to pursue other opportunities. Any relevant experience in your chosen area will be valuable in helping you make a transition to a new focus.

- **Start Your Side Hustle:** Begin working on your passion project on the side (evenings, weekends, lunch breaks). What steps can you take to get started?

- **Volunteer:** Find organizations you care about to contribute and see what help they need. Find something that aligns with the new skills you hope to build, or just get started doing something meaningful and see what unfolds.

- **Get More Training:** Research certification or graduate programs (online or in person) to build new skills. Always do the cost-benefit analysis of taking on loans or assuming debt to get the training versus learning on the job.

- **Do Research:** Start to gather more information to inform your choices. This could include reading articles and blogs, searching for jobs that sound interesting, checking out people or groups that fascinate you on LinkedIn, or listening to podcasts. Following leaders or influencers who are discussing issues that interest you is a great place to start, then you could reach out for informational interviews to learn more about these areas.

- **Teach Yourself:** Watch videos (YouTube is invaluable for this) or read articles and books about what you're interested in to learn new skills. LinkedIn now offers multiple training programs online, and open university curriculums are making more courses available. Research MOOCs (massive open online courses) that offer classes for free or at low cost.

- **Work Your Network:** Start cultivating relationships. Seek referrals, find companies that prefer internal candidates (so you can get your foot in the door, then transfer to other roles), or find ways to expand who you know so you discover what's going on in your chosen area.

- **Make Time for Your Job Search:** Most people pursue new opportunities while still working. This is an effective way to avoid income disruptions, though it can add additional stress around finding balance between your day job and a search process. Be intentional with your time.

- **Start a Creative Project:** Give yourself a personal challenge to start, build, design, or otherwise create something new that you've always wanted to do. This could mean picking up an old hobby or discovering a new one. Find something you love and go for it—you have no idea where it could lead. Creating art of any kind can spark new ideas.

- **Travel:** Consider taking a discovery vacation (or even a staycation, if budget is an issue). Explore new things to uncover different parts of yourself and start to see things in a new light. Experiencing other places and cultures will help you to become open to other ideas and possibilities.

- **Journal:** Writing about your thoughts, interests, feelings, and experiences is a wonderful way to unlock access to your unconscious psyche and reveal new insights. Consider starting a daily practice. If you don't like the idea of writing freehand, start an online document or speak out loud to your phone's voice recorder. The idea is to get your ideas out and see what emerges.

- **Take Care of Yourself:** Recognize what you need to stay optimistic and committed to your vision. If you are in between positions, make your health and wellness a priority. Detox from any unhealthy situations you may have left. Regain your sense of self as you informally engage with others. Pursue passion projects to refuel your tank.

- **Play the Long Game:** As I've shared, following a stepping-stone approach is an effective way to make changes over time. This requires being patient and developing one's skills. Job hopping is one way to move closer to what you want.

There are many ways to learn more about what you're interested in without having to get a full-time job or an advanced degree. Start with and follow your passions and interests. You can do whatever you want—and it can be fun, too. Why limit yourself? Find ways to practice doing what you want so you can learn as you go. Build a solid understanding of the principles, challenges, and relevant issues for what you care about to become more knowledgeable.

Clarify Your Focus

When connecting or sharing with others, communicate your chosen focus (around the specific job, function, company, industry, type of role, skills to use, or environment) to help others understand your goals. The clearer and more accurately you can articulate what areas you are interested in, the better. You don't need all the details pinned down, since your interests may evolve through your research and experience but explain enough so others can know where to direct you.

Here are two areas of interest to consider when evaluating your preferences. Understanding where you fit on the spectrums can help you align your preferences as these represent very different perspectives.

- **Quantitative versus Qualitative**
    - ¤ *Quants* prefer *numbers*. They enjoy focusing on performance, conducting data analysis, quantifying results, and measuring outputs. They often emphasize production and output over impact.
    - ¤ A *qualitative* emphasis is most concerned with *concepts* and understanding the big picture and strategy. This looks at

217

more in-depth factors to reframe issues within a broader context beyond metrics alone.

- **Specialist versus Generalist**
  - ¤ *Specialists* prefer to go *deep*. They enjoy developing in-depth knowledge to become a subject matter expert (SME) in a chosen area. Specialists may be highly valued in larger companies that require specific expertise, and they often work independently to develop their knowledge base. Specialists are not typically found within startups, unless their knowledge is essential to the business and they become the go-to person (for instance, around technology a company is selling).
  - ¤ *Generalists* like to go *wide*. They excel at many different things, easily taking on challenges. They often don't like to get caught up in the details, as they are bigger picture-oriented and can see the forest for the trees. Their skill set is often valued by smaller, more entrepreneurial organizations where they can become a jack-of-all trades, master of none. Generalist roles can sometimes be found in larger organizations starting new businesses or high-growth divisions that require active engagement across functions.

EXERCISE: Own Your Experience

You are all your unique cumulative experiences over time. Find the value of your backstory by weaving your life threads together into a beautiful tapestry that shows who you are and what you are capable of. Start by defining what you know and what you have learned from your experience. What lessons have you gained, and how does this translate into your knowledge, skills, and strengths now?

Create a storyboard or visual representation of your five most important life and work experiences and lessons. This can look however you want, whether a diagram, drawing, or PowerPoint chart. Consider responding to the following prompts, and then draw your experience or go free form with images, words, colors, or whatever speaks to you.

Depending on your personal style, feel free to use colored pencils, markers, or pens; type it up in a document; or graphically present it in a way that visually captures your experience. Consider creating a timeline or a treasure map portraying each of your experiences separately and then connecting how they relate to each other by highlighting certain themes.

The goal here is to do a download of all your skills within one visual frame, so you can see them and notice the trends and themes. You may have forgotten what you've done, or you may not realize how things fit together, until you step back and consider them from a new perspective.

For each of your five experiences (or more, if desired), reflect on the following areas, then fill in the below table.

EXPERIENCE	DESCRIPTION	LESSON	SKILLS

IMPACT	CARRY/ LIKES	LEAVE/ DISLIKES	WORDS	THEMES

- What label or *name* best captures that event? You can consider the formal title you had for the job, or the actual work you did or enjoyed doing (which may have been different). Examples are bank analyst (formal title) versus number cruncher (actual role), wildlife volunteer (role) versus being outdoors (what you enjoyed), summer counselor (role) versus mentoring and inspiring youth (function), or travel abroad (experience) versus cultural immersion (learning).

- How would you *describe* the experience? When you think of this situation, what words first come to your mind? Consider your experiences from additional perspectives—the company, people, lessons learned, or the nature of the experience itself. Sometimes, we loved the people, culture, or environment, but we had a difficult boss that prevented us from enjoying the work; or we loved our role, but we hated the organization.

- From each experience, what *lessons* did you learn?

- For the experiences, note which *skills* you used. Describe these in your own words, and if possible, consider different descriptive language that might relate to other types of work environments where these would be valued.

- Reflect on the *impact* of each important event on you (positive and/ or negative). How did it *define* you in any way? For example, did you develop new skills, face certain challenges, or grow in specific ways based on that experience? Certain experiences were pivotal in your life for different reasons, so it's important to acknowledge what you gained and how you may have evolved from each.

- What would you like to carry *forward* with you, if anything, from that experience? Which aspects did you *enjoy* the most? These are important things to look for in future opportunities.

- What would you like to *leave behind*? What did you *dislike* about the work? To the extent you can define what was not a fit, try to avoid these specific situations in the future.

- As you look at these different experiences, note any *words, themes, activities, or related aspects* of what you did. Were you working with people, numbers, things, or the outdoors? Which elements of the roles or organizational cultures most resonated?

What's Your Personal Brand?

The thought of branding can feel intimidating, uncomfortable, or yucky, if you associate it with being overly commercial, fake, or salesy. Looked at this way, branding implies the artificial creation of some unreal, constructed identity contrived to push product for a consumer-packaged goods company. While that is how some new products are designed, consider branding more holistically, beyond a productization perspective.

A brand is the impression formed by every experience and interaction with something, or someone, based on their unique essence. We all have a brand, whether we realize it or not and whether we have chosen to or not. People form opinions about who we are every time they meet us, just as we develop impressions of others based on how they make us feel.

Here are examples of various touch points or ways others interact with us, and how they might experience us through both our business or professional work and from our personal perspectives.

PROFESSIONAL BRAND	PERSONAL BRAND
• Website	• Meetings and conversations
• Sales team	• Elevator pitch
• Marketing collateral	• Online profiles (LinkedIn, Facebook)
• PR and media coverage	
• Social media	• Emails and follow-up
• Events	• Referrals and word of mouth
• Newsletters	• Social media
• Onboarding process	• Handshake and eye contact
• Leadership impressions	• Presence and energy
	• Portfolio and work

As the list shows, we interact with others in many ways, directly (in person) and indirectly (virtually online), influencing the opinions formed.

Do you know how you are being perceived? Often, we don't realize how we come across. While people respond to their intuitive impressions and actual experiences, you can change those perceptions by being thoughtful and intentional in how you position yourself. And you can change your positioning by intentionally shifting how you present yourself. The strategic choices you make about how you show up and interact, what you say, where you go, and which aspects of yourself you present all influence others.

Others unconsciously interpret our presence, and within under a second, assess who we are and what they think about us. We all respond viscerally to others and seek authenticity, as I've mentioned previously. Are someone's words, thoughts, actions, energy, and emotions in alignment? Perceived truth is the connection between our internal perspectives, values, and perceptions, and other people's external perspectives (how they experience us).

Your unique essence will always shine though, no matter where you are or what you are doing. Others form opinions, for better or worse, based on their reactions and experiences with us. So, while you can't control other people's perceptions, you can consciously choose how to present yourself to be the best version possible.

By radiating authenticity, you will attract people and opportunities interested in what you represent and have to offer. Essentially, like attracts like, and we become energetic matches for those who align with us. There's a scientific basis to this beyond the woo-woo. Researchers like Nikola Tesla focused on energy, frequency, and vibration; as did the famous scientist, Albert Einstein.

**Everything is energy and that's all there is to it.
Match the frequency of the reality you want,
and you cannot help but get that reality.
It can be no other way. This is not philosophy.
This is physics.**
—Albert Einstein

Realize you have more control than you might have imagined over many aspects of your life. You can start taking responsibility for the things you wish to change. The following practices offer some ways to think about how to bring your ideal self forward more. Take these in the spirit in which they are intended: to be playful, fun, and inspiring.

PRACTICE: Define Your Identity

Create Your Band Name and Hit Song
In speaking regularly to groups about personal branding, I have found most people relate to music, no matter their age, background, or experience. I relate music to branding on several levels:

- Musical genre can correlate with an industry or sector (for instance, heavy metal could be manufacturing, classical music could be technology, jazz could be creative design).

- Bands or artists are sources of inspiration (cue the symbol used by the singer formerly known as Prince), mentors or role models characterizing many different personas.

- Instruments symbolize different types of energies, or cultural experiences.

- Songs are compilations of different values and messages that present unique propositions.

Taking this one step further to show how it can relate to you, think of a favorite musician and their hit songs. What do you like about them and their music? What emotions do their songs evoke in you? What do you like about their style? What does their band name represent in your mind?

Now, it's your turn:

- *Create your own band name.* For fun, come up with a name that symbolizes who you are and what you stand for. This can incorporate your values, or any objects or creatures that speak to you.

- *Choose a song title that describes who you are.* For this, consider capturing aspects of your path or journey, affirmations, or what you hope to accomplish in your life.

Here's my example: Deep Spirit (my band) and "Finding My Groove" (my song). What does that tell you about me? If it wasn't obvious, I like to go deep spiritually, and I love dancing or anything that helps me to feel more embodied and empowered.

It's your turn to have fun with this. Don't overthink it. Think of this as a warm-up to get you out of your analytical mind to consider a different, more creative way of representing who you are and how you would like to be perceived.

Here are more ideas to get your playful creative juices flowing and to get your groove on.

- *Create your music playlist.* As Dick Clark once said, "Music is the soundtrack of our lives." Movies use music to powerful effect, from opening scenes that set the mood to tracks that capture the energy and spirit of each experience they want to create. Thrillers usually have edgy theme songs; or think of the visual storytelling and musical selections in James Bond films that convey a certain mood.

- *What would you like your life's musical soundtrack to be?* You might approach this exercise from a few different perspectives. What music inspires you right now? What represents where you are, what you want to create, and how you feel? Do you need new music or songs that speak to your heart and capture who you are and want to be? What mood can help you connect with your higher self? Playlists can be used to reflect all of these. Create your own musical compilations to get your juices flowing and light you up. Let the music help move and inspire you.

Note: Check out my Authentic Alchemy Path playlist on Spotify for some inspiration.

EXERCISE: Write Your Tagline

Knowing that branding can be lighter, take a stab at creating high-level positioning to capture who you are and want to be. A *tagline* is a one-sentence statement to position yourself in the minds of your audience, or another way to define your personal or professional brand.

Your personal branding will help others understand who you are, what you care about, and what you want to do. Clearly describing your background and/or expertise, what you're looking for, and how you add value provides greater context for others on where you fit. Combining your positioning statement with a call to action (or specific request, the "ask") creates your "elevator pitch," or a quick way to let others know how to support you based on what you are doing or communicating.

Your messaging should convey to others a clear objective that shares your focus and what you are seeking. Below is a sample statement with some additional examples below:

"My work as (your background, skills and/or experience) doing

X (the activity that you are interested in) makes me well-suited to meet your needs for Y (their needs)."

Describe your interests by explaining your contribution, your impact, and the space (industry, sector, impact, or challenge) you want to play in. Using your reflections above, create your own tagline. Draft a succinct, one-sentence positioning statement that clearly states who you are, your strengths, and your focus areas. Remember to capture who you are, what you've done, and the contribution you believe you can make.

Here are some examples:

- Hands-on problem solver redesigning high-growth business workflows

- People manager leading and aligning teams through ambiguity

- Fast learner who adapts to new situations with ease

- Experienced nonprofit leader driving the service economy

- Highly organized and accountable project manager delivering successful outcomes

- Creative visual artist designing bespoke berets

- Turnaround specialist solving tech startup challenges

- Social organizer turned efficiency expert

Step back from your day-to-day perspective and take a higher-level bird's-eye view to uncover points of connection between seemingly unrelated activities. All your experiences had a common connection point: *you*. Clarify how your experiences have been meaningful and led you on the path you've taken to date. Move beyond only focusing on job titles or specific functions or companies (unless this is exactly what you want to do), to consider the experiences and activities that tie them together.

- - - - - - - -

Values and opportunities can be closely related, such as making an impact, being part of a high-growth team, or working on an important mission. Once you see the relevant interconnecting drivers and motivators for you, it becomes easier to message your choices and why you made those choices.

Clearly, there was a logic (even if it seems fuzzy now) that drove your decisions at that time. It's okay; even if you might have made different decisions now. What's most important is to recognize and acknowledge what you learned from each experience, and to explain your choices now. Perhaps you enjoyed being at a company, until it got acquired and went from being small and entrepreneurial to large and bureaucratic; or, while you enjoyed a specific role, your style differed from your manager, so you moved to a new function at the same company but got stuck in a function that wasn't a fit.

What was your story? Understand and create a rationale for your previous choices to explain why your new approach makes sense now. Tell your story from the perspective of what drove your choices and how they relate. You may also wish to craft different messages to communicate with others depending on your interests and their backgrounds. Use these messages to support your talking points in discussions, and to structure your résumé and LinkedIn profile.

If you are unhappy with your previous choices, how might you recharacterize what you learned into a compelling directive for where you are focused now and why? You do not need to be a victim of your past. *Who you were before does not define who you are now or who you will be.* You can make different choices going forward, starting with how you choose to talk about yourself.

RITUAL: Tell Yourself Your Story

At night, or throughout the day, practice sharing the new version of yourself with yourself—either in your journal or in front of the mirror—and with others (partners, spouses, family, or close friends). Use your tagline positioning to share with more people and start believing it. Whether you simply remind yourself mentally or boldly state it out loud, keep reinforcing the version of yourself you want to be, so it becomes real and starts to reflect who you are.

Let's say you want to be more creative and develop your art. You might repeat the affirmation, "I am an artist." Then, you might share examples of your artwork, music, or writing with some close friends you trust. You could join a group or a maker community, take a skills-building workshop, or start posting your work on social media.

Your goal is to move from wanting (which can imply lack or scarcity) to doing (which implies ownership). Be the person "in the arena," as President Theodore Roosevelt said. Put yourself out there and come out of hiding. Take small steps to keep moving closer to being the artist you want to become. Even if you don't fully believe in yourself just yet, keep practicing. Notice how it feels and if things begin to shift as you start showing up differently.

Monitor the stories you tell yourself regularly. Lose the attachment to your old ways of thinking ("I'm not good enough"). Question your doubts. Are they still true? Shift the critical thoughts and messages into more positive affirmations. For example, if owning your full creativity outright feels like too much of a stretch, modify this to "My creative work and confidence grow stronger every day," to acknowledge where you are now.

Don't punish yourself or beat yourself up when you backslide; simply notice and move toward what you want. Recognize the discomfort, feel the fear, and choose to overcome your resistance to act and move closer to what you want. Keep focusing on your vision and why you are making these changes and doing this work.

REIMAGINE

CLARIFY and FOCUS
Continue your INTERPERSONAL WORK to evolve your vision and share it more broadly with others.

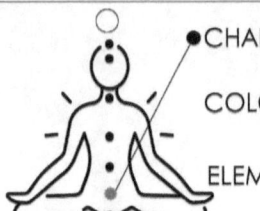

CHAKRA: Your SACRAL chakra is the source of your creativity and flow.

COLOR: Bight and powerful ORANGE strengthens your creative self-expression.

ELEMENT: WATER encourages movement and flow, the ability to evolve with change and connect with your intuition.

POWER ANIMAL:
HUMMINGBIRD can inspire you to find your soul's purpose and appreciate the sweetness of life.

CRYSTALS:

CARNELIAN can activate your fiery creative energy.

TIGER'S EYE is grounding, supportive and empowering.

TAROT CARDS:

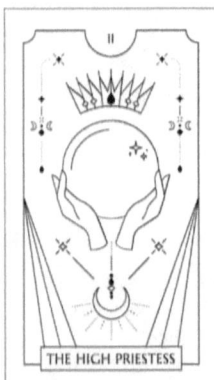

THE HIGH PRIESTESS

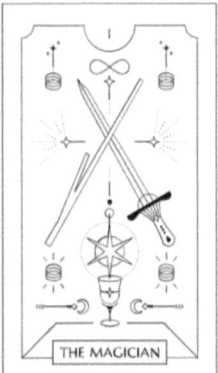

THE MAGICIAN

THE HIGH PRIESTESS represents deep trust. Let this card support you in following your inner knowing and using your intuition.

THE MAGICIAN has multiple tools available to empower you with many resources that can support you in manifesting your desires.

AFFIRMATION:

"I believe in and create new opportunities."

STEP 5: REIMAGINE

CLARIFY AND FOCUS

The process of changing one's identity impacts how we show up in relation to others, yet this evolution can unfold and transform subtly over time. Not only do we need to recognize that it's time to change (REALIZE), understand and let go of attachments to our old identities (RELEASE), determine how we want to be now (RECLAIM), and tell our new story (REFRAME), but we also need to start envisioning what is truly possible for us to create.

This new vision (REIMAGINE) fuels our fire to move forward toward our dreams. It connects with our sacral chakra, that source of our life spark, the inspiration and motivation that drives us to do the work of creating an exciting new way of being in the world.

The next story illustrates what can be involved in redefining how one shows up in the world and the possibilities inherent in reinventing oneself, even while doing the same things on the surface. We can continuously recreate and redefine ourselves in new ways.

CLIENT STORY: Soulpreneur Sovereignty

Casey, single and in her midthirties, was working with me to figure out her next steps professionally. She was wondering whether to continue her challenging consulting business (where she felt a huge responsibility to do everything) or take on a full-time job.

She was moving to Spain for a relationship and to pursue a dream of living abroad, but she was tired of dealing with difficult and demanding clients who were undermining her confidence—and underpaying her, to boot. Casey felt stressed-out, resentful, and overwhelmed by the emotional work and time required to support the business. She wondered whether and how to keep it going to retain her independence, or if she should look for something more stable and predictable.

While Casey appreciated the valuable experience she was gaining from her client projects, her working relationships weren't healthy or supportive, and in one case, it bordered on verbally abusive. Through our work together, she was able to step back and acknowledge how badly the clients treated her. She also could see how, by not pushing back or communicating her needs, her actions were allowing the poor behavior. However, with this awareness, she could start to shift the dynamic.

The stress had begun impacting her health and well-being. She was working more hours than she was paid for, undercharging for both her time and effort. She knew she deserved better and could no longer tolerate the toxicity. This was where inner work helped strengthen both her confidence and conviction.

Casey had to rebuild her self-esteem by recognizing and valuing her contribution to her clients' business outcomes. She raised her daily rates and changed her billing process to bring in income more consistently (biweekly instead of monthly). She was ready to stand in her power and firmly communicate these new requirements to her clients.

Casey also began more proactively managing her customers' expectations, and she started setting boundaries around her availability. She made it clear the terms of their relationship would be changing as she redefined the treatment she would tolerate going forward.

In learning how to engage in challenging conversations and set boundaries, Casey became more comfortable standing her ground. She found her voice and recognized her knowledge and contributions. As a result, her client interactions improved significantly, becoming more appropriate and respectful. She started earning more, and ultimately, she decided to fire the most difficult customer who paid her the least, freeing up her time for new opportunities.

Casey was able to take on new, more meaningful project work with clients that she loved, and she shifted her business dynamics overall. She had developed multiple strategies to manage her stress and business relationships more effectively. She continued using her strong communication and leadership skills to chart a new growth strategy.

" I could not have done any of the above, if I hadn't dedicated so much time, sweat, and tears to the care and development of my internal self. I continue to come back to what's within me (motivation, dedication, true commitment) to be able to do my work. It's more than dreams - it does feel awakening to be engaged with myself in this way. "

—Casey

The REIMAGINE step is about charting a new path and crafting a different vision that includes more joy, pleasure, free time, creativity, or whatever it is you need to feel more fulfilled. Creating this new reality requires you to own your gifts, appreciate yourself, and stop playing small. Prioritizing your own opinions, setting boundaries, and focusing on your own needs, rather than comparing yourself to others, will bring about more inner happiness. Putting your vision first helps you create more of what you want, care about, and enjoy.

Here are some ways to build momentum around your expansive new vision:

- *Who you are now is good enough.* You are exactly who you are meant to be right now. Stop comparing yourself to others, berating yourself for not achieving enough, or otherwise beating yourself up for being yourself. You are here to do great things and live a fulfilling life. That is the truth. You do not need to prove yourself. Perfectionism, and the desire to get everything right and in place, will only take you down and limit your progress. Choose to focus on the present moment, rather than look too far into the future.

- *Start from wherever you are.* You already have all the tools you need to begin moving forward in your journey right now. You may eventually decide that additional training, a degree, or a certification can give you some more credibility, but don't let that deter you from making progress or use that as an excuse to stop exploring. You can start moving toward your dreams right now, whether you choose to obtain further education or not—and you may discover on-the-job training or practical experience is enough for what you need.

- *Take care of yourself.* Make your well-being a priority and understand what creates safety for you. Revisit your specific needs and requirements (financially, energetically, physically, emotionally, etc.). If you are unemployed and need income, consider getting a job as your immediate priority to pay your bills and create more time and headspace to do further exploration. With more flexibility, your process can evolve gradually over time. Remember, there are no deadlines, time frames, or requirements around how fast your path will unfold. This is your journey, and it should be approached in your own way and at your own pace.

- *Take the next right action.* One way to avoid being overwhelmed is to focus on your immediate next steps. Choose up to three actions you can do now to move forward. While you may develop a longer list of activities to progress, identify your top three items for today or this week. This could include reading a chapter in this book and doing a reflection this week, then practicing something next week. Or reach out to three people to connect with and schedule a phone call in the coming week. Make your actions practical and focus on whatever will move you forward in the short term.

- *Do something new—anything.* Don't overthink your next step; the important thing is to get started and let it unfold. As you learn more, your clarity will increase. This will develop your focus and accelerate your progress. Start by picking one lane to drive in, and then you can decide whether to keep going in that direction or to switch lanes in the future. You may choose to explore multiple paths if that won't overwhelm you, and you can manage the variety while still making progress.

- *Experiment, adjust, and adapt.* Everything is a work in progress. With an open and curious approach, you can continuously assess how things are going and make changes as needed. Remember, your priorities are simply reflections of the choices you make. You can decide to change what you consider important as you learn more. Things don't need to be all or nothing. Consider this stoplight analogy in evaluating your options:

¤ **Red = Stop:** When things don't seem to be going your way, you feel unhappy, or you're not making the progress you desire, halt what you're doing altogether. You could take a break and leave your current job, relationship, or situation to free up time for something new. Ideally, think through the implications of any big decision by preparing, rather than simply reacting to your circumstances (by quitting, for example).

¤ **Yellow = Adjust:** Make subtle shifts or changes to your current situation. Build on what's working and try to minimize what's not working. For instance, modify your work hours, shift your energy toward the activities you most enjoy, or seek a new job within your existing company. Small tweaks can improve your existing situation without taking a huge risk.

¤ **Green = Go:** Decide to stay where you are and make things work within your existing situation, moving forward and continuing to build your skills. This recognizes the value of stability, security, and progress over time. Make slight adjustments on the margins by pursuing projects that align more with your interests or making space for personal hobbies outside of work to free up more personal time.

• *Track your progress.* Determine how you will measure success and assess what is and is not working. How will you know that you're moving forward? Are you excited about what you're doing and inspired to learn new things? Reconnect with your vision and values to revisit what flourishing would look like for you. When you find yourself getting off track, recognize that learning new things may also cause you to move in a new direction. Don't undervalue lateral shifts which can help you build skills, if you've gotten more clarity around what you enjoy and are still moving forward. Notice the growth in your confidence, clarity, and ability to feel more like yourself.

CHECK-IN: Clarify Your Focus

Hopefully, by now, you have identified a clear direction for your path and where you want to focus your energy in the short and longer term. In considering the stoplight analogy above, how will you move forward? Will you stay (green), shift (yellow), or leave (red) what you are doing now? Where, and how, will you direct your energy? What key activities have you chosen to direct your path? Can you clearly and succinctly summarize to someone else what you hope to do, so they would understand what you're doing? If not, no worries; this can be a work in progress.

Consider the following:

- *How can you develop more clarity around your vision?* How comfortable are you sharing your direction with others? Do they seem to understand where you are focused and what you are moving toward? If you struggle to articulate what matters, explore this further. Ask for feedback and input on what others hear you say. Where and when do you find yourself uncertain about your direction? What additional information could help you make a more informed decision? Who could you talk to for a new perspective or insight? Which additional resources could provide a different point of view and help you learn more?

- *Can you do fewer things deeper?* If you've been considering too many things without following through or doing anything well, you might get bogged down. If you feel overwhelmed or overextended, how can you simplify your focus? Could you explore one primary area for the next three months to see how that unfolds? Know that you can't please everyone all the time, nor can you be everything to everyone (then you are not special to anyone). If you've gotten distracted, remember to focus on what is most important to you.

- *How happy do you feel right now?* Pursuing your path should light you up. On a scale of one (low, uninspired, unenergetic) to ten (high, very inspired, energized), rate your enthusiasm now. If you are seven or below, what could you shift to raise your score? What do you really enjoy? How can you do more of that? If you are eight or higher, great—keep going in the direction of what you enjoy.

- *What steps can you take to align more with what you want?* Doing what you think you should be doing is not the same as pursuing what you love. How are you directing your energy? If you chose what matters most to you, would you spend your time differently?

You are here to do your thing. Keep coming back to your desires.

Avoiding Analysis Paralysis

If, like many of my clients, you are smart, intelligent, and thoughtful about your decisions, you also might get stuck in your head from time to time. One downside of over relying on your mind is becoming disconnected from the rest of your body. You can overlook additional valuable sources of inspiration, like insight, creativity, and knowledge from your heart, guts, and intuitive knowing. Can you balance the practical with the intuitive?

If you have multiple interests and skills, considering new possibilities can feel overwhelming because there are so many choices. Innovation and discovery require opening to explore and see what might be possible, stepping outside your comfort zone to take a risk and expand. In traditional marketing, uncovering the right place to be is called finding "product/market fit," and it's essential for new businesses to succeed. You are undertaking a similar process to uncover the sweet spot that aligns your interests, skills, and values with those who need and want what you have to offer.

Great ideas don't always find their exact audience from the outset. The classic product and business development launch process requires experimentation and discovery to understand the market needs, which leads to learning and adjusting in building a connection with the ideal audience. Consider a similar approach in pursuing your vision:

- In beginning your process, your goal is to *expand* your initial range of options, focusing on quantity and inspiration to generate excitement. When brainstorming, don't limit your choices too early, as you are generating ideas to keep a broad view of various possibilities.

- Upon considering this wider set of alternatives, start to *narrow* down your choices by exploring their benefits further. Gather information, weigh the pros and cons, and assess the practical issues to evaluate where best to put your energy.

- *Eliminate* whatever ideas don't feel like an ideal fit (for instance, if they don't match your values or priorities, or they require too many resources). Either remove these options completely or put them in a parking area to reconsider in the future.

- *Incorporate* the elements of different ideas that are interesting into what you want. You may select, merge, and integrate aspects of activities you explore to cherry-pick what you like from each.

- *Choose* your two or three best options that are most aligned with your interests, values, goals, strengths, and priorities.

- *Research* these even more deeply to learn as much as possible, then *refine* your focus further by following your interests and passions to determine what feels most aligned.

Regardless of what you ultimately decide or where you end up, remember that where you start is less important than the process of learning, adapting, and evolving. Also recognize that your process may be circular as you move in one direction, then circle back and incorporate things that you might have dismissed previously because you didn't have enough information or weren't sure how you felt.

Focus, Focus, Focus

Choosing one direction to move toward can be difficult for some individuals who naturally have a wide range of interests. Remember that you are not limiting yourself; rather, you are choosing an initial focus area that, by exploring more deeply, will reveal more information to help you move forward.

If this is you, reconsider your dream job and what you would absolutely love to do if money were no object. Begin with your heart's desire rather than shutting it down completely by imagining it's totally out of reach. Then, go back to Step 3 (RECLAIM, Part 2), to the "Leverage Where You Are" section for ideas on how to get unstuck. Remember, your goal is to conduct some experiments or have mini experiences to gain more insight.

With multiple paths, the key is to start somewhere and learn more about your focus, which then will lead to uncovering what is important to you.

<u>PRACTICE: Walk Your Talk</u>

The gap between what you want (in the future) and where you are now (present) can create insecurity if the distance feels too wide and uncomfortable to move forward. This, my friend, is your invitation to throw caution to the wind and start building your confidence to close that gap. One way to make your experience more tangible and real is by fully stepping into the new identity you want.

Begin answering these questions:

- *What identity do you want to claim?* Who are you? Refresh your personal brand to represent what you want, or revisit your tagline, even if it's aspirational, to try it on for size.

- *What words best describe how you wish to be perceived?* Choose three to five words that capture who and how you want to be seen. This approach to considering your brand or persona defines the energy for how you want to show up and be seen.

- *How can you own your new story?* Imagine yourself in the future, having realized your vision and looking back at where you are now. What did it take for you to get there? Do you need to act differently to step more fully into being this person now? Begin practicing in ways small and large. Will you wear other clothing, visit new places, structure your day differently? Which habits do you need to follow to be that person? What shifts could you make to become more of the person you want to be?

- *What symbolic object represents your dream or this aspect of your identity?* Consider a hat analogy: do you need to wear a different hat to step into your new role? Is it a baseball cap, cowboy hat, bandana, or visor? If hats aren't your thing, how about finding a new talisman, or one from earlier, to exemplify and encourage your new way of being. Could you create a mock-up of an award you would like to win, a diploma, a published article, or a TED Talk, as if it already happened?

Mark, an experienced professional who had been at the same company for many years, was struggling to consider his next career move. He felt frozen and unable to articulate the value of his contributions. He responded to my question about how he would like to be perceived and we created an affirmation statement and personal branding position to reflect exactly what he shared: "I am competent, confident, concise, clear, and consistent."

He would use this statement for inspiration and to measure how he was doing when he showed up. Was he acting confidently and competently? If not, what did he need to adjust? Was he as clear and concise as he could be, or was there room to improve? These key branding words and statement of purpose became a helpful reference point and metric to guide Mark's future actions and choices.

- *What additional practical, physical, and symbolic steps can you take to bring your dream alive?* If you want more money, write out a check to your name for that amount (for instance, $100,000), and keep it where you can see it. Keeping visual representations of what you want to create within sight can be powerful *(more ideas in the exercise below)*. Placing these reminders in spaces where you will regularly encounter them will call to mind what you care about and will reinforce your desires.

RITUAL: Conscious Career Creation Creative Collage

Let's bring your vision to life by creating a new definition of success. You are going to consciously craft a collage or visual representation of the work and life you want to create. Like making a vision board, this involves compiling images that speak to you and represent the life you want to create. While you can use your head to choose what you want, also incorporate your feelings and emotions to add an additional mood-board element with words, colors, and images (photos, pictures, drawings) that speak to you on an intuitive level.

Select different images (digital or print) that speak to you in some way, noticing whatever calls you and tickles your fancy. These might be photographs, colors, words, poems, or other objects. Either set aside time to do this in one sitting (thirty minutes to an hour), or gather images over time until you have enough to feel complete. Then, create the collage in a way that visually conveys your desires.

Printed versions can be done on any size paper with glue, or hard-copy images cut from magazines can be kept loosely in a folder. Digital layouts can be done with whatever software you prefer, to cut and paste graphics or create a personal collage with images that speak to you. How you bring everything together is up to you—whether in one master collection or a series of separate elements you can reflect upon in your journal.

Most importantly, have fun with this and make it your own. I have done variations of the above at different times, using Pinterest boards for visual inspiration, and copying images into PowerPoint slides with words or pictures grouped together around different themes (like money, lifestyle, health, travel, etc.). The sky is the limit around what this looks like.

Remember to think big and notice what you feel naturally drawn to. Let this process surprise and delight you as you connect with your feelings and true inner desires. Allow whatever is meaningful to come through by reflecting on what you truly want. Notice what feels most important and aligned with where you are right now and make the creative space for things to unfold in a more natural way.

It can be easy to set goals for what you think you should be doing or how you could be more effective. While focusing on a tangible goal can be motivating, it can be narrowly directed and create "pushing" and "striving" energy focused on "achieving." Consider a more inspiring approach by imagining how it will feel to explore what you truly desire, and then shift your energy toward that. Believe it can be that simple to choose more of what you want.

Notice any differences between the individual images and the impressions you get from seeing them all together. Reflect on what you have pulled together and notice how you feel and what drew you to your choices.

Do the images and words contain a story or insight for you? Is there a secret longing that's waiting to be expressed? Play with this process and make it yours. Let your imagination and creativity take over and see what wants to emerge. Notice how you feel throughout the process. Do you edit or judge yourself? Can you allow yourself to have whatever you like, even when it seems silly or frivolous?

Reflect, and make note of your insights. What did you notice about this process? What did you take away or discover about yourself that can support you as you move forward? For many of my clients, this exercise has been surprising and has revealed unexpected desires hiding below the surface. It can also reinforce important areas that you may want to pursue further.

PHASE 3:
OUTER WORK

REVEAL

ACT and CONNECT
Redirect your focus into the world by doing your OUTER WORK.

CHAKRA: Explore your inner power by strengthening your SOLAR PLEXUS chakra

COLOR: Brighten and enlighten your energy and strength with the color YELLOW.

ELEMENT: Let the FIRE element fuel your inner passion, purpose and transformation.

POWER ANIMAL:
Rely on the LION for inner strength and wisdom to trust yourself.

CRYSTALS:

CIRTINE is a powerful source of energy and manifestation.

AMBER is an earthy resin that is warm, nurturing and supportive.

TAROT CARDS:

THE EMPRESS

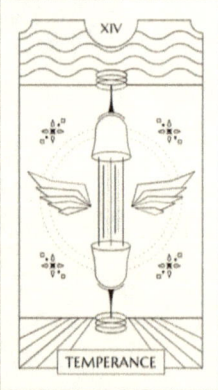

TEMPERANCE

THE EMPRESS encourages you to access your wisdom and step into your full power and knowing.

Find balance and flow within yourself and make informed and intentional choices with TEMPERANCE.

AFFIRMATION:
"I embrace my gifts, trust the universe and stand in my power."

STEP 6: REVEAL

ACT AND CONNECT

You are now ready to integrate all your work and complete your outer transformation in the REVEAL step, where you step out to live more fully from your truth. You are ready to show up from a place of authentic alignment. This step is connected to your solar plexus, the source of your power and gut instincts, so you will be moving into greater action to bring your efforts out into the world.

As you've no doubt been discovering, changes don't happen overnight, as much as you might want them to. Your internal awareness shifts, then you extend this and externalize your focus in connecting with others. The final outer step is fully embodying a new way of being. You have been undergoing your own unique process of determining how you want to live your life, likely expanding your definition of what is possible for your work.

Below is an example of someone who successfully integrated multiple aspects of his identity by making meaning from diverse experiences and redefined his work in the world by discovering a distinct path forward.

CLIENT STORY: Meaningful Work

Frank, an MBA student in his early forties, had a varied background that included previous work experience in

technology, consulting, hospitality, and ecotourism. He decided to pursue an MBA in Sustainability to switch careers into more meaningful work but was finding it challenging to uncover his path. He was frustrated by his progress and struggling to create the changes he desired.

As we reviewed his background, it emerged that he had been a chef, loved sailing, and spent significant time living on a boat. These unconventional interests were interspersed with more traditional roles, like consulting and tech sales. This conversation made clear that his true passions were food, clean water, and travel; yet he wasn't pursuing any of these interests in his desire to get a job. He was ignoring and overlooking his values and true interests to earn a living, assuming he couldn't find anything related to what he really cared about. Instead, I encouraged him to start actively pursuing his interests, and stop denying and hiding his background, to create a new path incorporating what he most cared about into his work.

He took this on board and began actively exploring how to integrate his interests and work. He secured an internship focused on food waste, then did a class consulting project exploring how to incorporate recycling into a large retailer's global supply chain. Through these experiences he was able to obtain another fellowship at the exact intersection of his passions: sustainability consulting to help a seafood company measure its carbon footprint and manage waste within its supply chain.

The fellowship was a positive experience for both Frank and the organization. While he was awaiting funding to continue the project and the important work he had started, he could see how the connection between his original passion for clean ocean water as a sailor and his work in making a sustainable impact aligned with his vision and values.

Creating something new and unique to your needs requires creativity, tenacity, and relationship building. While Frank acknowledged some frustration around the challenges ahead, he was committed to persistently pursuing the meaningful work he'd started and that he knew was needed to drive wider industry changes, recognizing his career was still a work in progress.

" One of my goals coming into the MBA in sustainability program was to get clear on the professional path I want to be on. Being clear on the industry, domain, and role that I want to be in avoids most of the uncertainty because I better understand what to say no to. Understanding what's important to me, what I'm good at, and what I enjoy is important in guiding my career choices. I would tell my younger self to ask for help. You don't have to do it alone. **"**

—Frank

Manage Your Mindset

An essential part of making your own success is believing that it's possible. Without personal examples, it can be hard to trust something intangible. Through experience, you will understand the terrain of your chosen focus area and make intentional choices about your path. Your commitment and trust in yourself, knowing you are moving in the right direction, will help you persist in the face of inevitable challenges that may arise.

249

Here are some reminders about how to stay optimistic, aligned with your vision, and consistent in approaching your process.

- *Change is an inside job.* Your personal growth reflects what and how you think and feel. Don't ignore or avoid challenges that arise. Try to remain positive when experiencing a setback, recognizing this challenge is meant to teach you something. Notice how, when, and where you give away your power by looking outside yourself and comparing yourself to others. Rember, you are doing this work for yourself, and this is *your path*.

- *Play to your strengths.* Don't underestimate your natural talents or take them for granted. Skills that come easily to you may not be natural for others. Double down on what you know you're good at, rather than building up your weaknesses. Of course, it's helpful to build your skills and develop areas that can support your growth and confidence but recognize that it's far easier to leverage gifts that will give you a competitive advantage.

- *You don't need to only do what you're good at.* Just because you can, doesn't mean you should. It doesn't mean you shouldn't, either. It's a choice. Embrace your skills that align with your interests, and notice when they are more of a fallback. Certain skills we develop, like people-pleasing or fixing other people's problems to validate ourselves, may cause us to act from a place of lack and scarcity. Beware of trying to make yourself feel better at your own expense. Rather, do what you want to do because it brings you joy.

- *Follow your passions.* Double down on the areas you care most about. Others will intuitively sense your enthusiasm and energy when you follow your natural interests. You will be far more knowledgeable about subjects you care about than those you force yourself to learn about because you "should." Positive attitudes inspire connection more easily than obligations.

- *Know what motivates you.* Intrinsic rewards (such as solving difficult problems, helping others, or finding unique or inspiring solutions) are often more compelling than extrinsic reinforcement (like higher compensation, a title, or an office). External signifiers can be important, but they lose their meaning and significance once obtained; then, you're on to the next goal without celebrating your accomplishments. Seeking validation from others will rarely leave you satisfied in the long term. Looking outside yourself for love, connection, and recognition will not fill your inner self. Consider whether insecurity is reflecting a core wound to be seen and addressed, rather than acted out.

- *Choose your environment.* Where we work (the space, location, energy, and our overall surroundings) impacts us deeply, and we often undervalue this aspect of our overall fulfillment. Do you feel at home, that you belong where you are—in the right place, physically, not just organizationally or metaphysically? Are you an East Coast or a West Coast person? Do you like big cities or rural countryside, or perhaps small towns or suburban areas with great schools to raise your family? Who do you want to surround yourself with? Do you need to be close to family? Moving from a city apartment to a country house with twice the space and green everywhere helped me understand how much space matters.

- *Find your peeps.* Choose the people you want to surround yourself with—warm, welcoming, and collaborative over cold, condescending, and competitive. Clearly, interpersonal dynamics create different experiences. The individuals you work with and for can be almost as important as your work itself, because enjoying your colleagues and feeling supported can shift

the dynamics of how you feel. We are all more interconnected than we realize, so recognize which aspects of who and where you work will support your desired outcomes.

Live (on) Your Purpose

To thine own self be true ...
—William Shakespeare

Hopefully, by now, you have a sense of who you are (your personality, strengths, and experiences), what you care about (your values, preferences, and dislikes), and how you like to work (your leadership style and ideal work situation). Recognizing your gifts, what is the impact you want to make? Have you acknowledged what you know and have learned to embrace a new vision for your life and work? How can you more fully ground in your truth? Let's reinforce your vision and bring it more fully into reality.

CHECK-IN: Create Your Ideal Work

In reviewing your previous reflections and what you've learned from your research and discovery process, what is most appealing to you now?

Consider the "creative brief," a document used to define exact specifications and operating parameters for design teams to develop and deliver successful outcomes. Who is the audience? What is the format? How should the message be communicated? These guidelines provide clear and specific constraints, setting limits and providing structure to inspire creative concepts that meet the core objectives and achieve the goals. Ideally, this avoids producing visually appealing ideas that look great on paper but don't deliver what is wanted or needed.

You have an opportunity to craft the creative brief for the life and work you want. *Write up your "ideal description" to capture the best possible work and life situation for you.* Define what you would like to be doing. Go beyond the traditional "job description" to consider how you most want to spend your time, without getting hung up on semantics or being limited by what others are doing. Write down all the elements that will bring you satisfaction:

- Which activities do you most enjoy? Describe your job function, role, and responsibilities.

- What does your work or job entail? Which tasks are most actively engaged in?

- What impact are you making? Who are your customers? What results do you deliver?

- Who do you work with and for? What is the culture? What is your boss's work style?

- Do you have your own business? What size organization do you work with or for, and are you part of a team or working independently?

- How are you spending your time? When does your day start? Are you at home or in an office?

- Where are you living? Will you be in the same location? Do you need or want to move?

- How much are you earning? What's your total compensation?

- What are your benefits (health care, vacation time, training, etc.)?

- How are you working (reading, writing, researching)? Are you independent or working part time?

- What type of company are you with? Where are they located? What are their values and work environment like?

By now, you should have a good idea of your preferences. If this seems challenging, do more research. Find twenty to thirty different jobs postings or other sources of inspiration (across social media, articles, Pinterest, etc.) to get started. Job boards like LinkedIn, Indeed, or specialized industry forums are excellent resources for examples of currently available jobs or individuals doing interesting work. See what sounds exciting to you. Note all the words, functions, and titles that jump out. What do they have in common? Do you notice any themes?

Go Deeper: Choose three jobs, companies, or people doing things you're interested in to find out as much as possible about them, their backgrounds, and their relevant skills. See what you discover. Is it worth reaching out to pursue a conversation or explore opportunities with them?

Now, reflect on your observations:

- What appealed to you?

- What did you notice? Were there any surprises?

- Which important concepts, themes, or ideas emerged?

- Were there any new roles or functions you hadn't considered before?

- What felt like a great fit? Where were you intrigued but thought it might be a stretch?

- What words and concepts do you need to capture and articulate?

- Where do you need to adjust your focus or how you describe what you're looking for?

Write up this inspiration for clarity around what appeals to you now. If possible, narrow your search to three possible job functions, roles, or possibly different titles in different industries. Do you have the skills for what you want to do? If so, start emphasizing them in your résumé and LinkedIn profile, and remember to mirror the language you've uncovered being used in your target market. If not, what skills will you need to develop or cultivate, and how might you get more training or experience in this area?

PRACTICE: Take Action

With this clear definition of where you want to be, what is needed to activate your priorities? *Define three to five actions you can take in the next week to move forward.* Schedule time in your calendar to do these things.

At the end of the week, review your progress in the following areas:

- What did you accomplish?

- How did you feel?

- What did you learn, and how can you apply this to your path?

- How did this help you move your vision and goals forward?

- What is the next natural step for you to take to build on what you've learned?

- On a scale of one (unhelpful) to ten (very helpful), how valuable was what you did? If you rated your efforts six or less, how can you become more effective and raise your score in the future?

- What is within your control to do differently?

Remember the power of three to simplify your focus without becoming overwhelmed. Remind yourself of the three most important areas to address and remember why they are important. This can be applied to your daily priorities, weekly tasks, and your monthly activities.

Focusing on the right activities will help you quickly progress toward your goals. Act with intention. Doing easy things to keep busy is not the same as doing important activities that produce more tangible outcomes. Busy activities don't always help you make progress. Neither does doing the right activities with the wrong mindset or doing unhelpful activities because you don't know what matters. Action does not always equate to movement or progress, while building on your successes to create momentum will help you continue to grow.

Envision the full picture of what you want to create, even if you don't know where every piece of the puzzle belongs. The story below illustrates one person's journey to find meaning at different stages of their life and work.

STUDENT STORY: Inquiring Minds

Many students pursue graduate school to advance their careers, though some are driven by a deeper motivation to learn and grow, both personally and professionally. Jacob was already in his forties upon entering business school, and he had a more unusual background than most, following three previous career changes.

After obtaining an undergraduate Bachelor of Arts degree in sociology, he garnered broad experience across a wide range of businesses. Several through lines played out across his journey that he often revisited as he would evaluate where to go next. Jacob was a musician and photographer, a passionate mindfulness advocate (practicing Zen meditation), and an avid reader and writer.

His initial job out of college was leading environmental programs for an apparel company. Jacob then pursued journalism to begin writing a series of sustainable guidebooks, evolving that interest in environmental journalism into hosting a podcast series. After eight years, he began a second career in media and entrepreneurship, as founder and cofounder of several startups connecting music, media, and art, leveraging his extensive writing experience into chief marketing roles.

After ten years in startup mode, he decided to take a radical, nomadic mid-career one-year sabbatical, during which time he planned to explore different interests to redirect his future life path. He considered social-emotional youth education, tenants' rights, consciousness training, and psychedelic therapies. Interspersed between those were interests in learning Spanish, writing a book, and pursuing his photography more. He also advised another startup and explored climate- and human-friendly buildings for a family real estate project.

Jacob codified a set of principles to guide his time off, found an accountability buddy, and traveled extensively. He actively structured his time by journaling and undertaking an in-depth study of his life to date, combined with yoga, exercise, and meditation. This gave him an opportunity

to deepen his spiritual practice and address some personal challenges more actively. I was particularly impressed by how he applied a thoughtful and rigorous analysis of his interests through the following mind map to understand all the elements that had impacted his path to date (industries, job functions, focus areas, and interests).

Following his sabbatical deep dive, Jacob decided to obtain a business degree in sustainability. He completed one year; then, after contemplation and personal reflection, he realized his interests were broader than the MBA, and he decided to move in a different direction rather than completing the full program.

Jacob chose to focus on the intersection of nonprofit community advocacy work through a youth organization that he had begun consulting for, which became an important jumping-off point for further growth. He Is now pursuing further training in nonprofit financial management and policy administration and expanding his interests in mindfulness and sustainability.

The second half and next chapter of his life and journey continues as he contemplates how best to make an impact. He is pleased with where everything led him so far because it feels fruitful and exciting, though he recognizes he is still in transition. He envisions standing at the foot of the mountain trailhead, unsure which equipment or team will help him reach the summit, but he is ready to trek forward with enthusiasm.

" For the past few years, I've had three guiding principles that I try to come back to when I face uncertainty: do my part to help the issues that matter

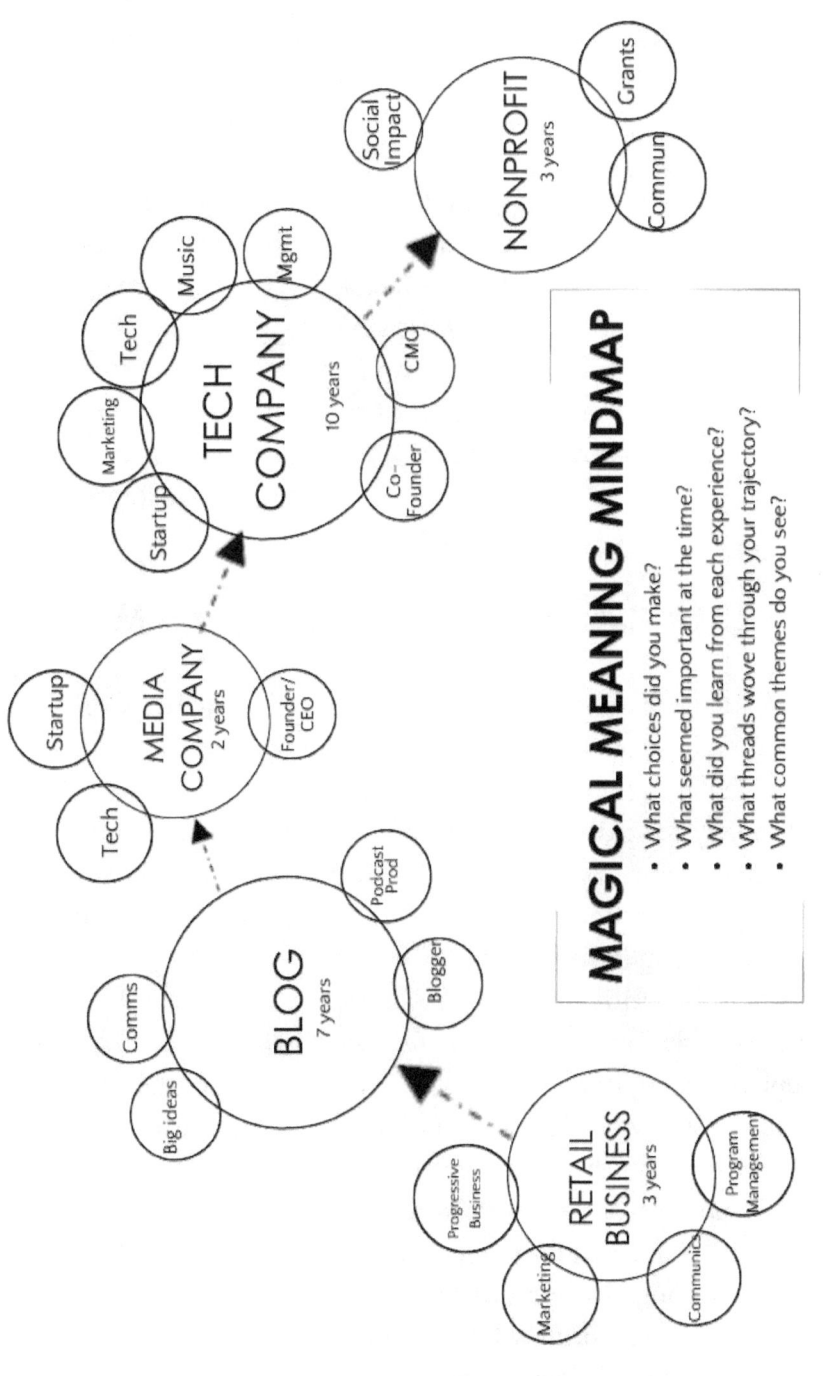

MAGICAL MEANING MINDMAP

- What choices did you make?
- What seemed important at the time?
- What did you learn from each experience?
- What threads wove through your trajectory?
- What common themes do you see?

most; cultivate and spread wisdom; be okay being a regular person. The first one is about building a career focused on having sizable positive impacts: building a panoramic view of the world, crafting a theory of change, and then deciding which pixels of the panorama you want to try and influence. The second one is about inner development, which for me means cultivating and exploring my connection to this magnificent universe and the web of life. And the third is a reminder to be humble. At the end of the day (and at the end of our lives) we're all just regular people, equally tiny and equally valuable. **"**

—Jacob

EXERCISE: Magical Meaning Mind Map

Refer to your vision board previously crafted in the Conscious Career Creation Creative Collage. Let's continue that creative thinking using a mind map, an organized visual representation of loosely related ideas connected by lines and common themes. A mind map is a powerful way to visually capture complex ideas simply and in one place, to see and play with the connections between them in new ways.

Start by writing one central concept in the middle, which you can encircle: for instance, *Me (or My Vision)*. Then, add related topics around this central circle to include important areas of your life and work. These could include home, well-being, career, family, free time, health, or whatever projects or aspects of your life are important. If you want to focus exclusively on work, related concepts could include boss, colleagues, compensation, benefits, job function, company, or industry. Within the secondary bubbles, add more details capturing what they represent with lines connecting those concepts. Following the theme above, for instance, under the job function, you could add all the activities you identified in the Create Your Ideal Work exercise above.

You can freehand draw topics, then add lines and connect new bubbles of all the things you're interested in personally and professionally; or find a software tool like Miro or MindMeister (which both have free versions) that automatically set these diagrams up for you. You could also create your own in PowerPoint.

See how Jacob, above, chose to approach his mind map which inspired this exercise. He used the diagram to begin mapping out his career path choices; highlighting important themes and interests in each of his jobs and seeing how they fit together which helped him to evaluate his next steps.

Ideally, you will capture as many details as possible without editing or limiting yourself, and you will have all of these within one master diagram. Use a large piece of paper or a digital space, and don't limit yourself. Typically, when I create a mind map, it naturally expands as I consider more options because it's a very effective way to simplify complex thoughts and group them together in creative, unconventional ways to uncover patterns.

Once everything is on one page, notice what came up.

- What did you choose to focus on?

- What was important to you?

- Did anything new emerge?

- How did it feel to see everything reflected in one place?

- Do you have a sense of what could be possible?

<u>RITUAL: Treat Yourself</u>

When undergoing change, it's important to positively acknowledge your work and progress. *What nice things can you do to reward yourself?* How can you consistently recognize your journey and forward movement? For instance, could you sit down to a fabulous tea or favorite coffee every morning before dedicating an hour to your path work? Could you take a luxurious bath in the evening to nurture your creativity, or go for a walk in nature to get away and be with your thoughts? Do you need daily recognition, or setting a specific goal that you acknowledge?

What do you need to be more of yourself? How can you prioritize spending time on your progress without forcing yourself to be different than who you are? Embrace what you need without blaming, shaming, or feeling guilty for being yourself. It can be as simple as appreciating yourself by creating conditions to excel.

Peter, a business professional who wanted to become a writer, kept forcing himself to wake up early in the morning to do his personal writing work, except that he wasn't a morning person. He was most creative and energetic late at night, but his inner assumption and judgments had him believe the smartest people did their work in the morning. After realizing how he was beating himself up, we discussed changing his schedule. Peter decided to give himself permission to begin working at night, and almost miraculously (but not altogether surprisingly), he became much more productive while working at his own rhythm.

Another introverted client, Jeri, became easily distracted working in an open office. She was more productive when working from home or wearing headphones in the office to concentrate when surrounded by others. Eventually, she recognized how her current job was working against her natural style. She decided to find opportunities where she could be more productive that suited her preferred way of working. Knowing her style and needs meant Jeri no longer needed to fight against herself, her role, and her organization. She could just be herself and feel more capable and supported in her work.

Imagine creating your life on your own terms. This is what is possible as you keep pursuing more of what you love and create work that reflects everything that matters to you. Now, you get to bring it all together.

REAP

BE and DO YOU
Complete your process by fully integrating all your efforts and bringing together your OUTER WORK.

CHAKRA: Connect to a higher source through your CROWN chakra.

COLOR: Embrace your regal nature with PURPLE.

ELEMENT: ETHER represents lightness of being, connection to source and higher purpose.

POWER ANIMAL:
Let EAGLE's power inspire you to soar above any challenges and gain a higher perspective.

CRYSTALS:
AMETHYST is a powerful healing and nurturing stone that supports your growth.

LEPIDOLITE can support you in finding inspiration and deeper connection to yourself.

IV

THE EMPEROR

TAROT CARD:

Let THE EMPEROR be a source of wisdom and inspiration. This extremely powerful card within the major arcana invites you to recognize your mastery. Realize that you are ready to stand firmly in your leadership and full embodied power.

AFFIRMATION:

"I readily share my talent and gifts with others."

STEP 7: REAP

BE AND DO YOU

By now, you have more insight into what you want to do and where you can excel. It's time to start benefiting and bringing yourself more fully into the world through the REAP step, by connecting with your crown chakra, the source of your higher knowledge and wisdom.

As you've likely experienced, change doesn't happen overnight; yet big shifts to find more meaning, purpose, and alignment can occur with effort and commitment. Jace's story below demonstrates a successful transition where persistence paid off when they committed to a vision even while there was uncertainty.

CLIENT STORY: Intentional Career Crafting

Jace, an MBA student, outlined their career progression over two years, including their decision-making process, for me to share their evolution and thinking below.

"I started my career with an undergraduate degree in Film, spending ten years working on film sets in the creative media industry), mostly freelancing, and various full-time engagement positions. Throughout the later years, I began to feel disconnected from the work while a desire to create more impactful change emerged.

"I knew I needed to first start back in a more structured position. I eventually moved into Sales for a cinema company, which was supplementary during the pandemic, though I had never done sales and wasn't interested in it. As I continued to consider the type of impact I wanted to make with my work, I eventually decided to pursue sustainability.

"When I started my sustainability business graduate degree, I was unclear about my sustainability direction or what I was interested in. To get a foot in the door, I took a job in partnerships at a nonprofit that was focused on food waste and the multifamily housing sector. It did not feel like a fit and I have since removed the experience from my résumé, not only because it was short-lived, but also because it represented more sales experience, which I was no longer pursuing.

"During school, I realized that I connected most with impact finance, and I decided to pursue this because I found inspiration in affordability relating to the local economy. I then decided to pursue more internship and contract experience to further transition me into sustainability, rather than going for a full-time job (because of my current lack of experience in the finance/sustainability world). I got an ESG Consulting summer internship focused on ESG compliance and green building certifications in the built environment. Simultaneously, I took on a freelance project for a professor evaluating regional flows of capital, which gave me more experience in finance and how capital is moved to support marginalized entrepreneurs in those communities.

"When those internships ended, I needed something more financially stable and was offered a Senior Manager position *at a building energy management consulting company focused on energy-efficiency projects, energy analysis, and local law compliance in the built environment. Even though this was a return to sales and things I was less interested in, it was a crash course in energy, consulting, policy, capital projects and the housing space. I overall am a better professional because of this position, and it has been a valuable addition to my résumé and credentials.*

"During this time, I was taking a yearlong consulting class, and I chose to do this work with an impact investment firm focused on underserved farmers and ecological stewardship. I chose this to enhance my experience and résumé with more impact finance experience.

"To continue pursuing impact finance positions that were not sales focused, I applied for multiple internships/fellowships and was accepted into a competitive fellowship program, and I chose a project that was a good combination of my previous experience and future experience building, and it gave me the opportunity to grow my practice and understanding of the impact finance space.

"I had initially debated whether to accept this fellowship because I wanted to make sure it was enough of a pivot from my full-time job to make leaving worth it, but I ultimately decided that another impact finance project and the prestige of the fellowship would be a great next step in leveraging my experience toward my career goals. Simultaneously, I completed a specialized finance certification outside of my degree program to sharpen my hard skills and continue to build my résumé.

"The threads I see are:

267

- *The nonprofit's housing focus helped me get the ESG Consulting internship (in the built environment).*

- *The freelance project enhanced my résumé and finance credentials.*

- *Those three experiences signaled to the building energy management company that I would be a fit for the Senior Manager position.*

- *All four of these experiences plus my consulting class project were to my benefit when applying to the fellowship.*

- *Taking an outside finance certification has also given me leverage in interviews.*

"It hasn't all perfectly gotten me to where I want to be, but the journey isn't over. Taking the small opportunities to build experience has led me to make a successful transition, and I believe more folks could benefit from this approach. Another pro tip is that I include all the names of my courses on my résumé, which I believe helps me get through AI résumé screens because of the course keywords.

"Hopefully, the journey will continue toward my ultimate goal of a full-time position in Impact Finance!"

- - - - - - - -

Some valuable lessons from Jace's experience are:

- *Be willing to explore different work opportunities to gain valuable experience.*

- *Increase your knowledge, confidence, and self-awareness through continuous skill building.*

- *Leverage your existing background to make a move to more aligned companies.*

- *Build momentum with the stepping-stone approach to keep growing and moving forward.*

- *Explore multiple avenues to gain experience (classwork, certifications, internships, projects, freelance, full-time work).*

- *See the through lines, or "threads," to effectively message how to present your background.*

You are ready to reap and be yourself. Find safety, and ground within. Define what enough means to you.

<u>PRACTICE: Be and Do You</u>

Fully and authentically integrate all your progress uncovering your truth and what lights you up into all aspects of your life and work. Align your thoughts, actions, words, emotions, and energy to sync these elements; it's a constant process of coming back to yourself and your intentions.

Create your updated vision and manifesto by reflecting on these questions:

- *What* is important to you?

- *When* do you feel most yourself (happiest, confident, calm, centered)?

- *Who* do you care about and want to surround yourself with?

- *Where* are you most comfortable being?

- *Why* does your work matter?

- *How* do you want to feel and show up in the world?

Return to this vision and values by centering yourself, staying connected to your path and soul purpose. Use this chapter's affirmation, or create your own, to regularly state out loud and remind yourself. What else might you need to learn or do to support your growth? Do other aspects of your life need shifting or tweaking to incorporate more of what will fulfill you? What can you do to embody yourself even more fully?

Regularly consider this ongoing exploration. You have the power and tools to make any necessary shifts, so what processes will support your continuing growth?

CHECK-IN: Reflect on Your Process

Reinforce your growth by remembering the lessons you've learned and how they have impacted you. How will you take this knowledge forward and transform it into your wisdom? Take a few moments to consider the process you've undergone throughout this book.

- *What have you learned about yourself throughout this journey?*
    - ¤ What did you already know?
    - ¤ What was new and surprising that you discovered?
    - ¤ What were the biggest shifts you noticed?

¤ How do you feel about yourself now?

¤ Do you like or love yourself more?

- *Where are you still challenged or less enthralled by your progress?*
  - ¤ Can you acknowledge any discomfort without judging or making yourself wrong?
  - ¤ Is it okay that some things may not have happened as you expected?
  - ¤ How can you make progress on the areas you want to develop further?
  - ¤ With the spirit of continuous improvement, what growth opportunities exist where you are now?

- *What is your current vision, and how has it evolved?*
  - ¤ Did you revisit and refresh your original vision?
  - ¤ How has it changed? What has been most significant for you?
  - ¤ What's true for you now that you didn't realize was important?
  - ¤ What are your desires and nonnegotiables?
  - ¤ Are you excited about your path?

- *How can you incorporate your vision into all aspects of your life?*
  - ¤ What steps could you take daily, weekly, monthly, quarterly, or annually to stay on track?
  - ¤ How will you continue your discovery process to support your ongoing reinvention, transformation, and growth?
  - ¤ What will help you stay motivated and inspired?

EXERCISE: Celebrate You and Your Progress

Acknowledge all the work, both challenging and enjoyable, you've done to get to this point. Too often, we hurry past our achievements,

quickly moving on to the next thing on our list. Slow down and appreciate what you have accomplished so far. Gratitude is a state of being, and it creates more things to be grateful for.

Plan your own mini celebration to mark your following through on the commitment you made to go on this journey and your willingness to see where it might take you. What are you most proud of? How will you honor all you've achieved and how you've grown?

Find some activity (large or small) to note this occasion and treat yourself. Here are some ideas:

- **Plan a Vacation:** What exciting destination, day trip, staycation, or weekend getaway can encourage you to explore and adventure?

- **Buy Yourself a Treat:** Is there something large (like a new technology tool) or small (like your favorite ice cream) that could be meaningful and pleasurable?

- **Get Out in Nature:** Go for a walk or hike, head to the beach, or sit in a park.

- **Make or Create Something:** Paint a picture, do some craft, or build something that is meaningful for you (a new talisman to signify your achievement).

- **Buy a Special Memento:** Find a new plant, crystal, or piece of jewelry that you love.

- **Have a Fabulous Meal:** Cook or go out to a new local restaurant for fun.

- **Get a Spa Treatment:** Go for a massage or ask a partner to give you one.

RITUAL: It's Your Party!

Let's get this party started! For many cultures, and in my shamanic tradition, major life milestones are recognized as important rites of passage. Key life events often occur during periods of transition from one state to another (for instance, from childhood to adulthood, getting married, or losing a loved one). Acknowledging important occasions is a meaningful and powerful way to support individuals undergoing life changes. We often celebrate these events symbolically through rituals that mark their significance.

How can you honor what you've achieved? What recognition do you need to celebrate yourself? Could you do something personally meaningful, like write yourself a letter or create a work of art? What speaks to you? You could put on some beautiful music, dress up, or cook a special treat. Friends and guests are optional, though having others acknowledge and celebrate your achievements with you can be worthwhile. Set aside time to make this important ritual your own.

You deserve to be celebrated for your work as you step into your power and share your gifts. Let me be the first to congratulate and see you. I see you, and I honor your growth!

THE WORLD

CONGRATULATIONS!

YOU'VE DONE IT!

The World card in tarot represents the conclusion and successful completion of the current phase of your journey. It is the final card of the major arcana, indicating the culmination of this current growth and development cycle before a new process starts again. Know that you have reached an important milestone, though your journey will continue as you learn more, evolve, and make new choices about your future.

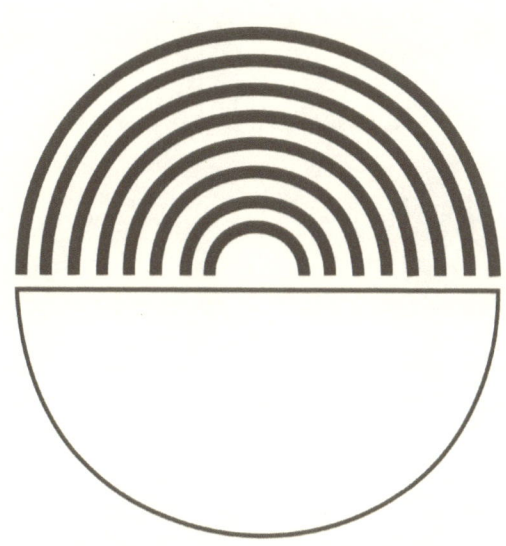

CONTINUE: YOUR ONGOING JOURNEY

POSTSCRIPT

Nine different book drafts had accumulated in my file folders over the past ten years. They were all variations on what is shared here, but none in this form. Clearly, I wasn't ready to write those versions, since it wasn't the right time. Things happen for a reason when they are meant to. This is the book that I was meant to write, and I'm excited to share it now, since it represents the culmination of all my experiences, training, insights, and personal integration process to this point in time. It's exciting to mark its completion and add "author" and "elder" to my list of qualifiers, so I can share my wisdom more broadly.

- - - - - - - -

Similarly, your work is the result of all your experiences that will continue to blossom over time as you grow, learn, and deepen your knowledge. Your path is to own, share, and disseminate your unique wisdom and gifts.

What's Possible for You?

Doing deep inner work can bring many rewards—financially, emotionally, physically, spiritually, and energetically. Clearing resistance to change and overcoming challenges. Finding more fulfillment, purpose, and meaning through work. Developing strategies to navigate challenges and uncertainty. Becoming empowered to make smart life choices to bring yourself more joy and ease.

Many of my clients have been promoted, stepped into leadership positions, started or grown their businesses, and earned more money. While these are all legitimate reasons to grow professionally, short-term achievements rarely bring long-term satisfaction. We all desire more financial security and stability; yet, we mostly want to live and speak our truths, to be ourselves—fully, completely, and without guilt or shame. We want to live our values and find places and spaces to be ourselves and make positive impacts on others and the world.

This is not easy work. Facing your fears and bringing out your essential gifts takes courage to pursue your passion. I celebrate the many lessons you have learned, whether small or profound, in your process. My intention was to guide you to more joy and satisfaction in doing what you love without worrying about what others think.

How will you take your work out into the world and pay it forward? What wisdom are you meant to share? Did you discover a new purpose, create change in your existing organization, or decide to start your own business? Were you able to create more balance in your life, make more time for travel and personal interests, or leave a toxic environment or workplace to discover a new way of working? Make note of each accomplishment as the victory it is.

Please share your wins with me on Instagram *@lenorekantor* and *#authenticalchemypath*. I would love to acknowledge your success!

Dive Deeper

Pursuing your path may have uncovered challenges that feel difficult to face alone. Additional coaching guidance can support vulnerable inner work within a safe container. An unbiased external source can also offer a useful sounding board for exploring new ideas and navigating unanticipated challenges. You can become too close to your own experience to appreciate what may be happening and how you are reacting to your circumstances. Additional perspective can provide other possible choices. Healing support can be particularly valuable to address trauma or release old, repetitive patterns.

Should you have friends with a shared desire to pursue their purpose, you may wish to start an Authentic Alchemy Path Circle to work through your process together (find more resources at *www.authenticalchemypath.com*), or join one of my coaching programs.

Additional information is available at *www.growthwarrior.co*.

Pulling It All Together

My intention through this guidebook was to help you transform your thinking about your life and work. I hope your passions emerged and have become woven into your purpose. The Authentic Alchemy Path offers a lifetime of transformation as you continue to step into your gifts.

Continue to cultivate your unique talents as you let them take you in the direction of your heart. Follow your dreams. Listen to the inner stirrings that nudge you and ask for your attention, for they are guiding you in the right direction. Ignore them at your peril. Know that the long and winding path will continue to unfold as you step forward. May every day bring you a new discovery.

You can continue your work and connect further here:

- Use the *So, What Do You Do?* companion workbook to record your journey and reflections (find more information at www.growthwarrior.co)

- Invite Lenore to speak about transformation, personal growth, professional fulfillment and The Authentic Alchemy Path by reaching out here: *info@growthwarrior.co*

- Sign up for regular inspiration and insights in Lenore's e-newsletter here: https://bit.ly/GrowthWarriornews

- Find additional book resources through Lenore's website at www.growthwarrior.co/ or directly at www.authenticalchemypath.com

- For more inspiration, follow Lenore on:
  - ¤ LinkedIn (https://www.linkedin.com/in/lenorekantor/)
  - ¤ Instagram (https://www.instagram.com/lenorekantor/)
  - ¤ Facebook (https://www.facebook.com/growthcoach/)

- Find out how transformational coaching with Lenore can support your personal and professional growth by scheduling a discovery call here:
  https://calendly.com/growthwarrior/discovery

ADDITIONAL RESOURCES

This guidebook has been informed by multiple sources, several of which have been compiled and presented below. Included are some references that have influenced my work, and/or ideas referenced within the book, and which may be helpful for your journey. This is not intended to be an exhaustive compendium, but rather a list of resources and information that I have found valuable.

Mindset

- **Creativity:** *The Artist's Way* (Julia Cameron); *Big Magic: Creative Living Beyond Fear* (Elizabeth Gilbert)

- **Money:** *The Soul of Money: Reclaiming the Wealth of Our Inner Resources* and multiple other books (Lynne Twist)

- **Nonverbal Communication:** Albert Mehrabian (extensive research on the connection between words, thoughts, and intentions)

- **Personal Growth:** Abraham Maslow's Hierarchy of needs (theory of individualism and the prioritization of needs)

- **Power Poses:** Amy Cuddy (TED Talks on body language)

- **Workplace Satisfaction Research:** *How Americans View Their Jobs* (Juliana Menasce Horowitz and Kim Parker, Pew Research Center, https://www.pewresearch.org/social-trends/2023/03/30/how-americans-view-their-jobs/) and "The World's Broken Workplace" (Jim Clifton, *The Chairman's Blog*, https://news.gallup.com/opinion/chairman/212045/world-broken-workplace.aspx?g_source=position1&g_medium=related&g_campaign=tiles)

Psychology

- **Attachment Style:** Bowlby and Ainsworth (research and theories on anxious versus avoidant reactions to separation and fear of abandonment)

- **Flow State:** *Flow: The Psychology of Optimal Experience* (Mihaly Csikszentmihalyi), happiness is not a fixed state but can be developed as we learn to achieve flow in our lives

- **Gratitude and Positive Psychology:** Martin Seligman and others (research on gratitude)

- **Growth versus Fixed Mindset:** Carol Dweck

- **Impostor Syndrome:** Pauline R. Clance and Suzanne A. Imes

- **Internal Family Systems:** Richard Schwartz and parts work

- **Relationships:** Jim Rohn (you are the average of the five people you spend the most time with)

- **Resiliency and Grit:** Angela Duckworth

- **Values:** Authentic Happiness: Values In Action (VIA) Test (University of Pennsylvania), register, then click on "Questionnaires" and take the VIA Survey of Character Strengths here: https://www.authentichappiness.sas.upenn. edu/testcenter (then select test from the Engagement Questionnaires section)

- **Values and Shame:** *Dare to Lead* (Brené Brown), list of values (https://brenebrown.com/resources/dare-to-lead-list-of-values/) and TED Talks on shame

- **Visualization:** Research on the reticular activating system

Physiology/Somatics

- **Chakra System:** *Eastern Body, Western Mind: Psychology and the Chakra System as a Path to the Self* (Anodea Judith)

- **Epigenetics:** *The Biology of Belief* (Bruce Lipton)

- **Human Energy Field:** *Hands of Light* and other books (Barbara Brennan)

- **Intention:** *The Intention Experiment: Using Your Thoughts to Change Your Life and the World* (Lynne McTaggart)

- **Interpreting Stress:** Kelly McGonigal (TED Talk and research on stress as good for you versus bad)

Spirituality
(Shamanism, Tarot, Mythology, Feng Shui)

- **Crystals:** *Connecting with Crystals: Crystal Wisdom and Stone Healing for Body, Mind, and Spirit* (Laurelle Rethke)

- **Decluttering:** *The Life-Changing Magic of Tidying Up* (Marie Kondo); *The Gentle Art of Swedish Death Cleaning: How to Free Yourself and Your Family from a Lifetime of Clutter* (Margareta Magnusson)

- **Feng Shui:** *School of Intention* programs and podcast (Dana Claudat)

- **Mythology:** *The Hero's Journey* (Joseph Campbell), *The Heroine's Journey: Woman's Quest for Wholeness* (Maureen Murdock)

- **Personal Development:** *Empowerment: The Art of Creating Your Life As You Want It* (David Gershon & Gail Straub)

- **Shamanism:** *Shaman, Healer, Sage* (Alberto Villoldo and The Four Winds Society); Foundation for Shamanic Studies and Core Shamanism (Michael Harner)

- **Tarot Counseling and Alchemy:** *An Introduction to Transformative Tarot Counseling: The High Art of Reading* (Katrina Wynne)

- **Tarot Resources:** Multiple books by Mary Greer and Rachel Pollock; MotherPeace deck

- **Therapeutic Tarot:** *Tarotpy: It's All in the Cards* (Lauren Z. Schneider)

- **Traditional Chinese Medicine:** *Wood Becomes Water: Chinese Medicine in Everyday Life* (Gail Reichstein)

ACKNOWLEDGMENTS

I honor the Earth and universal guidance that has supported me on this journey.

I am grateful to all the individuals pursuing personal and professional growth that I have been fortunate to guide to more fulfillment and truth. I would like to personally thank the clients and students whose stories have been shared here (pseudonyms protect their confidentiality). I believe their experiences offer beautiful lessons and reflect universal themes.

I have had so many mentors, teachers, and supporters throughout my journey who have crossed my path. Many were advocates who shared their deep wisdom and knowledge, taught me new ways of being, and appreciated my potential. I am particularly grateful to Ann Bradney (Radical Aliveness), Dana Claudat (School of Intention), Florencia Fridman (Cacao Lab ceremonial cacao training), Phil Weisberg, Mark Elmy (The Four Pillars Mayan cosmovision), David Gershon and Gail Straub (Empowerment Institute), Dr. Eban Goodstein (Bard's MBA in Sustainability), Laurelle Rethke (crystal healing), Katrina Wynne (professional tarot counseling), Alberto Villoldo (The Four Winds), and the Foundation for Shamanic Studies (multiple teachers). Too many gifted practitioners to mention have coached me and I am grateful for how each has supported my personal and professional journey, healing, and growth.

With deep gratitude, I appreciate the friends and peers who shared their insights around the book. Thank you, my book support team: Libby Dubick, Gisela Garrett, Laura Hartley, Menachem Tabanpour, Mavis Rhodes, Linda Frank, Liza Pullman, Sherry Chilton, Anna Krusinski and Victoria Heath Silk. A heartfelt thank you to Elham Ali, Jacob Gordon, Josée Guévremont, Stacey Jewell, Sarah Miller, Fredrick Selby, Catherine Tedrow, Jason Titus and Kelly Wallace for their input.

I would like to thank Canva for providing the stock graphics used to create the mystical reference visual guides, including the tarot cards, animals, crystals and elements images © through sketchify @ canva.com).

This book has been its own beautiful learning journey, and I appreciate how it has allowed me to know myself better and be guided to exactly what was meant to be.

I greatly appreciate my thoughtful partner, Guillaume Gantard, who has been a constant source of love and support.